W9-CEW-179

Polar
Explorations

Other titles in the World History Series

Polar
Explorations

Don Nardo

LUCENT BOOKS

A part of Gale, Cengage Learning

GALE
CENGAGE Learning™

Detroit • New York • San Francisco • New Haven, Conn • Waterville, Maine • London

GALE
CENGAGE Learning™

LIBRARY OF CONGRESS CATALOGING-IN-PUBLICATION DATA

Nardo, Don, 1947-
  Polar explorations / by Don Nardo.
    p. cm. -- (World history)
  Includes bibliographical references and index.
  ISBN 978-1-4205-0360-9 (hardcover)
  1. Polar regions--Discovery and exploration--Juvenile literature.
  2. Explorers--Polar regions--Biography--Juvenile literature. I. Title.
  G580.N2 2011
  910.911--dc22

                                                    2010039667

Lucent Books
27500 Drake Rd.
Farmington Hills, MI 48331

ISBN-13: 978-1-4205-0360-9
ISBN-10: 1-4205-0360-X

J910.911
Nardo
15 Apr. 2011

Printed in the United States of America
1 2 3 4 5 6 7 15 14 13 12 11

Printed by Bang Printing, Brainerd, MN, 1st Ptg., 03/2011

Contents

Foreword

Each year, on the first day of school, nearly every history teacher faces the task of explaining why his or her students should study history. Many reasons have been given. One is that lessons exist in the past from which contemporary society can benefit and learn. Another is that exploration of the past allows us to see the origins of our customs, ideas, and institutions. Concepts such as democracy, ethnic conflict, or even things as trivial as fashion or mores, have historical roots.

Reasons such as these impress few students, however. If anything, these explanations seem remote and dull to young minds. Yet history is anything but dull. And therein lies what is perhaps the most compelling reason for studying history: History is filled with great stories. The classic themes of literature and drama—love and sacrifice, hatred and revenge, injustice and betrayal, adversity and overcoming adversity—fill the pages of history books, feeding the imagination as well as any of the great works of fiction do.

The story of the Children's Crusade, for example, is one of the most tragic in history. In 1212 Crusader fever hit Europe. A call went out from the pope that all good Christians should journey to Jerusalem to drive out the hated Muslims and return the city to Christian control. Heeding the call, thousands of children made the journey. Parents bravely allowed many children to go, and entire communities were inspired by the faith of these small Crusaders. Unfortunately, many boarded ships were captained by slave traders, who enthusiastically sold the children into slavery as soon as they arrived at their destination. Thousands died from disease, exposure, and starvation on the long march across Europe to the Mediterranean Sea. Others perished at sea.

Another story, from a modern and more familiar place, offers a soul-wrenching view of personal humiliation but also the ability to rise above it. Hatsuye Egami was one of 110,000 Japanese Americans sent to internment camps during World War II. "Since yesterday we Japanese have ceased to be human beings," he wrote in his diary. "We are numbers. We are no longer Egamis, but the number 23324. A tag with that number is on every trunk, suitcase and bag. Tags, also, on our breasts." Despite such dehumanizing treatment, most internees worked hard to control their bitterness. They created workable communities inside the camps and demonstrated again and again their loyalty as Americans.

These are but two of the many stories from history that can be found in the pages of the Lucent Books World History series. All World History titles rely on sound research and verifiable evidence, and all give students a clear sense of time, place, and chronology through maps and timelines as well as text.

All titles include a wide range of authoritative perspectives that demonstrate the complexity of historical interpretation and sharpen the reader's critical thinking skills. Formally documented quotations and annotated bibliographies enable students to locate and evaluate sources, often instantaneously via the Internet, and serve as valuable tools for further research and debate.

Finally, Lucent's World History titles present rousing good stories, featuring vivid primary source quotations drawn from unique, sometimes obscure sources such as diaries, public records, and contemporary chronicles. In this way, the voices of participants and witnesses as well as important biographers and historians bring the study of history to life. As we are caught up in the lives of others, we are reminded that we too are characters in the ongoing human saga, and we are better prepared for our own roles.

Important Dates at the Time

ca. 320 B.C.
Pytheas, an ancient Greek explorer, writes a book describing his voyage to the Arctic region.

1610
English ship captain Henry Hudson sails toward the Arctic in hopes of finding the Northwest Passage.

1588
Spain launches the Spanish Armada, a huge war fleet, against England.

1620
A group of English settlers, the Pilgrims, land at Plymouth, in what is now Massachusetts.

1576
English explorer Martin Frobisher lands on Baffin Island, not far south of the Arctic Circle.

| 500 B.C. | A.D. 500 | 1500 | 1600 | 1700 |

A.D. 476
The last Roman Emperor is forced to vacate his throne, marking the official end of the Roman Empire.

1729
Danish-born Russian naval officer Vitus Bering discovers the strait separating Siberia and Alaska.

ca. 980–990
Groups of enterprising Vikings establish settlements in Greenland, near the Arctic Circle.

1773
British naval officer James Cook becomes the first person to cross the Antarctic Circle.

1776
Britain's thirteen American colonies declare their independence, thereby creating the United States.

of the Polar Explorations

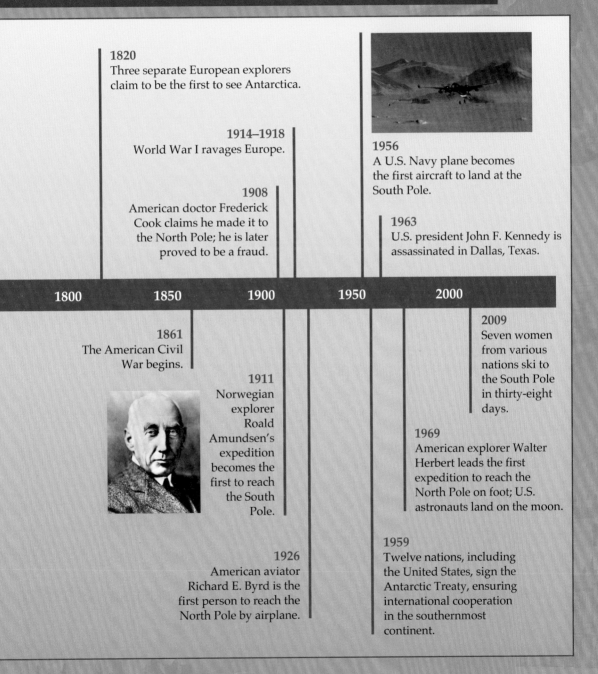

1820
Three separate European explorers claim to be the first to see Antarctica.

1914–1918
World War I ravages Europe.

1908
American doctor Frederick Cook claims he made it to the North Pole; he is later proved to be a fraud.

1956
A U.S. Navy plane becomes the first aircraft to land at the South Pole.

1963
U.S. president John F. Kennedy is assassinated in Dallas, Texas.

1800   1850   1900   1950   2000

1861
The American Civil War begins.

1911
Norwegian explorer Roald Amundsen's expedition becomes the first to reach the South Pole.

1926
American aviator Richard E. Byrd is the first person to reach the North Pole by airplane.

2009
Seven women from various nations ski to the South Pole in thirty-eight days.

1969
American explorer Walter Herbert leads the first expedition to reach the North Pole on foot; U.S. astronauts land on the moon.

1959
Twelve nations, including the United States, sign the Antarctic Treaty, ensuring international cooperation in the southernmost continent.

The Attraction of the Poles

For countless centuries, Earth's polar regions have existed for the most part at the seeming boundary between the real world and the human imagination. The North Pole and South Pole lie far away from the familiar sights and sounds of civilization. They are not only distant but also cold and desolate places visited by only a handful of rugged individuals in history and seen by most people only in photos and film clips.

Perhaps because they are so inaccessible and so unlike what the majority of people are used to, the poles have consistently proved compelling, even haunting. Books and movies about expeditions to these vast, frozen regions have been and continue to be highly popular. Part of this appeal stems from the ability of the poles to inspire and produce classic heroes. Throughout recorded history, a few hardy souls in each generation have felt the allure of what many have called the "ends of the Earth." Of the numerous unexplored regions on the planet's surface, the poles were among the last and most challenging to reach and chart. They were also among the most dangerous and claimed the lives of a good many of these intrepid voyagers. Indeed, the hazards, perils, and death tolls of polar expeditions have unarguably been part of the enduring fascination for these inhospitable places. In the words of Oxford University scholar Sarah Moss:

> The far north and south are places of death, where heroes go to test their heroism to its sublunary [earthly] limits. More than that, they are places where the limits of heroism are recorded, written into the landscape, and into the body, and onto the notebooks or the wax tablets that lie beside the body [of the fallen hero]. Polar places are

black-and-white landscapes in which the great explorers prove themselves, and us, by fighting on to the bitter end, striving, seeking, finding, and not yielding even to death itself.[1]

Why the Poles Are Cold

Such men and women who were, and remain, willing to risk injury and death by plunging headlong into the polar wildernesses have had various motivations. Some have done so to open up new trade routes to enrich their native lands; others braved the extreme cold and relentless desolation to expand human knowledge and advance the march of science; still others headed for the poles for more symbolic reasons—to increase their personal reputations or the status of their home nations. Finally, some polar explorers were driven mainly by the tremendous challenge of facing and defeating the most extreme and taxing physical conditions the planet can dish out.

Indeed, to experience the extreme conditions that exist at the poles was the incentive for most such expeditions. Furthermore, far fewer explorers would have died if the polar regions were not markedly more unsafe than nearly anywhere else in the world. In terms of geography, terrain, climate, temperature, plants and animals, and even trying to tell time, the top and bottom of Earth are virtually unique. Some have called them alien environments that happen to exist on our own home planet.

A good example of the atypical and in some ways bizarre nature of the polar regions is the manner in which time becomes warped and eventually meaningless within them. Everywhere else in the world time zones determine what time it is in various countries and cities. Those zones are defined on maps by lines of longitude, drawn vertically from the North Pole downward to the South Pole. In most places these imaginary lines are hundreds of miles apart. But they all get closer together and converge at the poles. As a result, no time zones exist at those two spots on Earth's surface. One's watch will still work there, but it is still impossible to tell what time of the day or night it is.

The polar regions also markedly differ from other places in the world because their extreme locations on the top and bottom of the globe limit incoming sunlight and thereby affect their climates. Earth rotates once daily on its axis, which is like a huge invisible rod that passes through the middle of the planet from north to south. The places where that imaginary rod touches the surface on opposite sides of the globe are the geographic poles. (These should not be confused with the magnetic poles. The magnetic North Pole, for instance, is the spot on the planet's northern surface where its magnetic field points vertically downward; that pole slowly changes location over time due to activity in Earth's core.) The region around the geographic North Pole is called the Arctic, while the area around the geographic South Pole is known as the Antarctic.

Each of these polar regions is defined on maps by a large imaginary circle that scientists call a line of latitude. Lines of latitude, which cross lines of longitude at right angles, are drawn parallel to the equator, which goes around the center of the planet from east to west and lies at 0 degrees latitude. The Arctic Circle lies at about latitude 66° north, or 66 degrees north of the equator; the Antarctic Circle lies at about latitude 66° south, or 66 degrees south of the equator. (The North Pole itself rests at latitude 90° north and the South Pole is situated at latitude 90° south.)

Because the polar regions that lie within the Arctic and Antarctic Circles exist at the top and bottom of the world, they are colder than most other areas on Earth. For most of the year, the bulk of direct incoming sunlight strikes the equator and the temperate latitudes located just above and below it. Meanwhile, the polar regions receive sunlight much more indirectly, making their climates colder.

The extreme locations of the poles also affect the apparent movement of the sun in those regions. Instead of rising and setting each day, at the North Pole the sun stays permanently above the horizon during the summer months and permanently below the horizon during the winter months. The same situation occurs at the South Pole, only in reverse.

Although the poles are both cold due to the minimal amount of sunlight that reaches them, in general the Antarctic is colder than the Arctic. This is because the southern polar region lies on a continental land mass 1.3 times the size of Europe. Called Antarctica, it is covered by ice and snow, which reflect much of the already indirect incoming sunlight. In contrast, the northern polar region lies in the center of an ocean (the Arctic Ocean). Its waters, though very cold by human standards, absorb and store a certain amount of heat from the incoming sunlight. Thus, average temperatures at the North Pole are -30°F (-34°C) in the winter and about 32°F (0°C) in the summer; whereas at the South Pole temperatures average -72°F (-58°C) in the winter and -15°F (-26°C) in the summer. Needless to say, such low temperatures, combined with shifting ice floes, frequent howling winds, unexpected storms, and phenomenally rugged terrain, make any and all human expeditions into these regions extremely difficult and dangerous.

The Treacherous Arctic

Of these dangers, shifting ice has taken a particularly awful toll on the explorers who sought to conquer the Arctic. The north polar ice sheet floating in the Arctic Ocean averages about 10 feet (3m) thick. This is more than enough to support the weight of men, sled dogs, and supplies. However, that ice is in an almost constant state of flux as it drifts along in the powerful currents flowing through the ocean. This moving ice can easily close in around a ship. For many centuries the vessels of the polar explorers were made of wood, and many were crushed by the shifting ice. Such was the fate of the *Princess Charlotte*, a nineteenth-century

If it were not for the extreme conditions that exist at the Earth's poles, explorers would not have readily gone there and certainly fewer of them would have died.

wooden vessel that got caught in Arctic ice in Melville Bay (in northwestern Greenland). According to a contemporary account:

> The steward had just reported breakfast ready when [the captain], seeing the [ice] floes closing together ahead of the ship, remained on deck to see her pass safely between them, but they closed too quickly. The vessel was almost through, when the points of ice caught her sides abreast of the misenmast, and, passing through, held the wreck up for a few minutes, barely long enough for the crew to escape and save their [life]boats. [The] poor [captain] thus suddenly lost his breakfast and his ship. Within *ten minutes*, [it] disappeared beneath the [water's] surface.[2]

One reason that a lot of ships were lost in this manner is that numerous explorers insisted on braving the dangerous waters surrounding and flowing through the polar ice cap. The few natives making up the permanent population of the lands within the Arctic Circle had long before learned to play it safe and stay near their respective coastlines, which lie several hundred miles from the pole. For a long time a majority of these natives were Native Americans, primarily the Inuit (Eskimo). They dwelled (and still dwell) on various Arctic islands or the Canadian landmass and interacted with the Vikings, Dutch, English, and other European explorers who entered the region over the centuries. Today, eight countries own inhabited or uninhabited lands within the Arctic Circle—Sweden, Norway, Finland, Russia, Denmark, Iceland, Canada, and the United States.

Antarctic Wonderland

In comparison, the Antarctic has never had any permanent residents, mainly because of the region's excessive remoteness and bitterly cold climate. Today, the only people who live in Antarctica are a few scientists who work in bases constructed and maintained there at considerable yearly cost. Hailing from numerous nations, none of which owns the southernmost continent outright, they come and go as their research duties dictate.

These periodic visitors to the South Pole encounter a markedly different physical terrain than that of those who live in or visit the Arctic. Scholar David Mountfield explains:

Almost all the mainland of Antarctica is covered with a permanent ice-cap, which is in some places more than a mile deep [and contains 90 percent of the world's ice]. This ice-cap, pushing ever outwards and down, extends beyond the land to form the great ice shelves that border the sometimes invisible coastline of the continent along nearly half its total length.[3]

Another way that Antarctica differs from its polar opposite in the north is that the southern continent has many mountains. Some are quite tall. Highest of all is the Vinson Massif, rising 16,000

The continent of Antarctica contains many mountains. The highest one is Vinson Massif, which rises to sixteen thousand feet.

feet (4,890m) into the sky. In addition, several of Antarctica's mountains are active volcanoes, which produce spectacular eruptions on a semiregular basis.

The combination of mile-deep ice (1.6km), coastal ice shelves, towering peaks, erupting volcanoes, and the absence of time zones, all engulfed in a never-ending deep freeze, make Antarctica a veritable geological and visual wonderland. Not surprisingly, it still lures researchers, nature enthusiasts, and sportsmen alike, while the northern polar region draws these same sorts of people for its own reasons. The mighty, ongoing attraction of the poles was well summed up by the late, noted English polar historian Clive Holland, who said about the North Pole:

There is a mysterious magic in standing at that particular place that has long beguiled [hypnotized] mankind. A century ago brave men died trying to get there. And nowadays tourists pay tens of thousands of dollars to be taken there by icebreaker. . . . They are happy to delight in the immense beauty of the rest of the Arctic Ocean, with the delicate blue-green tinges of the . . . ice floes driven together by immense forces of wind and current. [Getting] to the North Pole is just as irresistibly enticing [and] romantic. [For] some of those explorers who vied with one another to get there first . . . it was the most important thing in life.[4]

Chapter One

The Earliest Arctic Voyagers

From the earliest times, Europeans wondered what lay beyond the horizons that defined their familiar world. Those who planted colonies on Africa's fertile northern coast, for example, frequently speculated about what exotic lands and peoples might lie south of the vast, forbidding barrier of the Sahara Desert. In ancient times rumors abounded, including some that claimed that central Africa was inhabited by cave dwellers who lived solely on snake meat. They competed, it was said, with people with no heads, whose mouths and eyes were attached to their chests.

In contrast, for ancient northern Europeans—the future English, Irish, Dutch, Germans, and Scandinavians—rumor and conjecture centered most on what strange lands might lie farther north. They knew little about them for sure, but seemed certain that the farther one traveled northward, the colder it got. Occasionally, stories were told by travelers whose boats had been blown off course and into the frigid northern waters. They told about bizarre winters in which the sun never appeared; vast sheets of ice covering both land and sea; and spectral colored lights dancing across the night sky (now known to be the aurora borealis, or northern lights). Thus, the realization was passed verbally from generation to generation that a strange, desolate wilderness lay beyond the northern limits of the "known" world. As Oxford University scholar Sarah Moss puts it:

> In the Western imagination, the Arctic has always been a strange and beautiful place just over the horizon, just out of sight of the outer reaches of the continents, just off the edge of most of our maps. It lies there, close, part of the geographic imagination, and yet beyond familiarity, out of reach of

... culture and society. From the beginning of anything that might be recognized as European culture, the Arctic is present ... yet known only for its strangeness and inaccessibility.[5]

Only a relative few ancient and medieval Europeans had the rare combination of motivation, resources, and raw nerve required to venture north and enter what later came to be called the Arctic. Some of these explorers have likely been forgotten. They presumably include those who never returned from their fateful voyages or whose exploits never got recorded and passed on, either orally or in writing.

To Thule and Beyond

Of those earliest Arctic voyagers, the first whose journey and exploits were recorded for posterity was a Greek named Pytheas. He lived in the late fourth century b.c. in the city of Massalia, which had earlier been established by Greek immigrants on the coast of what is now southern France. At the time, Massalia was part of a vast Mediterranean-European trading network that stretched as far as Mesopotamia and Arabia in the east, Egypt and Nubia in the southeast, and Britain and Scandinavia in the north. Among the many goods traded, one of the most valuable was tin. Mixed with copper, it produced bronze, the ancient world's most versatile and widespread metal alloy.

The problem was that Europe had extremely meager supplies of tin. Most of it came from traders who claimed to know the location of the so-called tin islands, mysterious places supposedly located in the Atlantic Ocean somewhere beyond Spain. These were merely rumors, however, probably purposely spread to keep the location of the tin mines a trade secret. In reality, most of the tin used in that era came from northern France and southern Britain.

Pytheas somehow got wind of the truth and decided to try to open a direct tin route between the Mediterranean cities and Britain. He first crossed France (then called Gaul) on foot. Upon reaching the Atlantic coast, he purchased or rented a small ship, sailed north, crossed the English Channel, and landed in Cornwall, in southwestern Britain. At that point he likely hired local guides to help him locate the tin mines in the area.

Pytheas did not stop there, however. Maybe because he heard that more mines filled with tin and other metals existed in the British Isles, he moved on in an ever-widening journey of exploration. Sailing up the western coast of Britain, he reached Scotland. From there, he visited the Orkney and Shetland islands, the latter lying about 170 miles (280km) north of mainland Britain.

Thereafter, Pytheas's movements became more difficult to trace. But it seems that he likely went next to the Faroe Islands, situated roughly halfway between Scotland and Iceland. A number of modern scholars think he then proceeded to Iceland, called Thule by the Greeks and Romans, and beyond, crossing the Arctic Circle. This supposition is

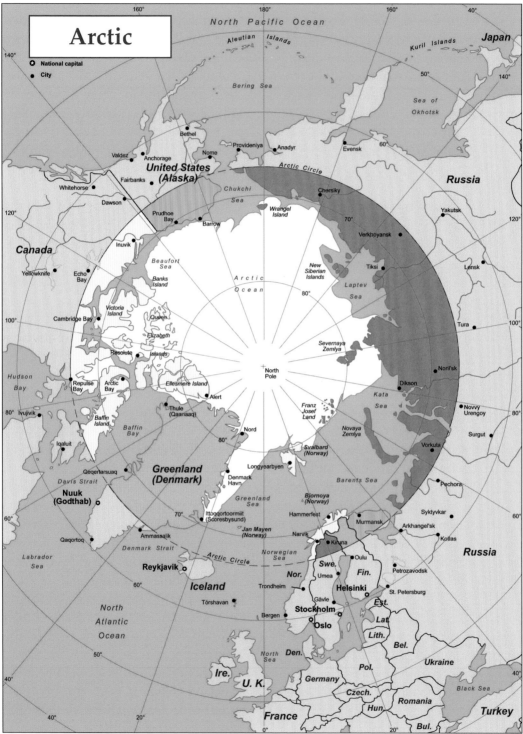

Map of the Arctic Circle.

based on certain remarks Pytheas made in a book titled *On the Ocean*, which he wrote in about 320 b.c. after his return to Massalia. Regrettably no copies of the volume itself have survived. However, at least eighteen ancient writers mentioned, discussed, and quoted from it. Among them was the Roman scholar Pliny the Elder, who said, quite accurately it turns out:

> Because the sun approaches nearer to the top of the world on summer days . . . the parts of the Earth that lie at the poles have continuous daylight for six months at a time and continuous night for six months when the sun has withdrawn in the opposite direction towards midwinter. Pytheas of Massalia writes that this happens in the island of Thule, six days [by boat] north of Britain.[6]

The final legs of that Greek's historic journey can be reconstructed to some degree from a review of all the surviving quotes and paraphrases from Pytheas's lost book, plus the commentary on them by other ancient authors. After leaving Iceland, Pytheas appears to have sailed into Arctic waters. Why he did so remains unknown. Perhaps by this point he was driven less by economic incentives and more by pure scientific curiosity. In any case, he eventually encountered the southernmost edges of the vast northern polar ice cap, which at the time extended a few hundred miles farther south than it does today. Forced to turn back, he eventually made his way back to Britain and from there to the more temperate Mediterranean.

Searching for Solitude

Historians wonder why other Greeks, and/or later the Romans, who conquered the Greek lands in the last two centuries b.c., did not follow up on Pytheas's northward voyage. If they had, perhaps the entire history of Europe and the world might have been different. However, no such follow-up expeditions came during the remainder of ancient times. National Geographic Society researcher Anthony Brandt explains why:

> Later [ancient] writers and geographers often did not believe [Pytheas] even while they described what he had to say. Much of what we know about his discoveries comes from sources calling him a liar. And nobody in the classical [Greco-Roman] world followed him north. The Romans were conquerors, not explorers. The phrase "ultima Thule" . . . representing the last place on earth, comes from the Roman philosopher and playwright Seneca, who in *Medea* puts into the mouth of one of the characters this prophecy: that at some time in the future, "when the earth is older," explorers will find new continents. "Then Thule will no longer be the last land." But no Roman showed any interest in going to this Thule that Pytheas had discovered. When

the Romans got to Britain, they stopped short of Scotland and built a wall [Hadrian's Wall], to keep the barbarians out. They had gone far enough north.[7]

As a result of this failure to follow in Pytheas's footsteps, after the collapse of the western Roman Empire in the fifth and sixth centuries Europe largely forgot about the islands lying near and inside the Arctic Circle. They needed to be rediscovered, and they were. This time the explorers hailed from medieval Ireland and Scandinavia. First came a group of intrepid Irish monks led by one named Brendan, who was later recognized as a Christian saint. They were driven neither by financial motives nor scientific curiosity. Rather, the monks wanted to escape what they viewed as the too crowded and busy towns of the British Isles and to find more remote lands where they could pray and meditate in peace, quiet, and solitude.

To this end, in about a.d. 500 or so, Brendan and his fellow monks launched some small, hide-covered boats known as coracles (also curraghs). Somehow these wobbly, unreliable craft proved seaworthy enough to carry the monks along Pytheas's route. Leaving Scotland, they sailed and rowed to the Orkneys and then to the Shetlands and Faroes. From there, according to surviving stories about their voyage, they took a hint

Testing Pytheas's Claims

Writing in the fourth century b.c., the Greek explorer Pytheas claimed he had sailed past Iceland and encountered vast sheets of ice, now surmised to be Arctic pack ice. Many modern scholars think his account is largely true because other claims Pytheas made have proved to be accurate. For example, after sailing along Britain's coasts, he estimated the mileage of the island's circumference. Although his book has not survived, the first-century b.c. Greek historian Diodorus Siculus cited that estimate in one of his own writings, saying: "Britain is triangular in shape, but its sides are not equal. . . . Of the sides of Britain, the shortest, which extends along Europe is 7,500 stades [850 miles (1,368km)], the second, from the Strait [English Channel] to the [northern] tip is 15,000 stades [1,700 miles (2,736km)] . . . so that the entire circuit of the island amounts to 42,500 stades [4,740 miles (7,628km)]." Modern scientists have determined that Britain's coastline is 4,548 miles (7,322km) long. That is very close to Pytheas's estimate, suggesting that he did not exaggerate his claims.

Quoted in Barry Cunliffe, *The Extraordinary Voyage of Pytheas the Greek.* New York: Walker, 2002, p. 96.

from migrating birds. As former Royal Geographic Society historian L.P. Kirwan tells it: "Living in monasteries [in Britain], they had seen how each year at the first sign of spring, flock after flock of wild geese migrated northwards to summer breeding grounds, and it was probably by following the flight of these spectacular and noisy birds that the Irish monks reached Iceland."[8] It may be that even distant Iceland was not remote enough for some of these churchmen. Evidence suggests that they eventually sailed on to Jan Mayen Island, located 300 miles (483km) farther north.

Erupting Volcanoes and Giant Icebergs

That Brendan and his companions made it to Iceland and into Arctic waters seems well supported by various passages in the *Voyage of St. Brendan the Navigator*. This early medieval narrative was copied, recopied, and translated repeatedly for centuries, producing several surviving versions. The story contains numerous obvious exaggerations and fabrications, largely giving it the feeling of a fable. However, the following excerpt is hard to interpret as anything else but an ongoing eruption of one of Iceland's many volcanoes:

On another day there came into view a large and high mountain in the ocean, not far off, towards the north, with misty clouds about it, and a great smoke issuing from its summit. . . . Afterwards a favorable breeze caught the boats, and drove

This thirteenth-century manuscript page of an account of Brendan's voyage depicts one of the many fantastic adventures he supposedly experienced.

them southwards; and as they [the monks] looked back, they saw the peak of the mountain unclouded, and shooting up flames into the sky, which it drew back again to itself, so that the mountain seemed a burning pyre.[9]

Similarly, another passage clearly describes a giant iceberg, indicating that the monks had traveled well north of the Arctic Circle:

One day [the monks] saw a column in the sea, which seemed not far off,

St. Brendan Sees an Iceberg

In the legendary account describing the northward voyage of the medieval Irish monk Brendan, he and his companions witnessed a large object they called a "column." A number of modern experts say it may have been a giant iceberg with an ice bridge and a passage the monks could sail through.

St Brendan ordered the brethren to take in their oars, and to lower the sails and mast, and directed some of them to hold onto the fringes of the canopy, which extended about a mile from the column, and about the same depth into the sea. When this had been done, St Brendan said: "Run in the boat now through an opening, that we may get a closer view of the wonderful works of God." And when they had passed through the opening, and looked around them, the sea seemed to be transparent like glass, so that they could plainly see everything beneath them, even the base of the column, and the skirts of the canopy lying on the ground, for the sun shone as brightly within as without.

Quoted in Denis O'Donoghue, trans., *Voyage of St. Brendan the Navigator*, Lampeter, UK: University of Wales, Lampeter. www.lamp.ac.uk/celtic/elibrary/translations/nsb.htm.

yet they could not reach it for three days. When they drew near it St Brendan looked towards its summit, but could not see it, because of its great height, which seemed to pierce the skies. It was covered over with rare canopy, the material of which they knew not; but it had the color of silver and was hard as marble, while the column itself was of the clearest crystal.[10]

Whatever objects or islands the Irish monks witnessed beyond Iceland, the very fact that they risked so much and worked so hard to reach them is telling. It demonstrates that, like many other people throughout the ages, they viewed the polar region as a distant, solitary place, far beyond the beaten path, so to speak, of civilization. As Moss points out, for them these were positive rather than negative attributes. They viewed the Arctic, she says,

as the ultimate place for retreat and reflection. . . . The idea of the Celtic hermitage, an isolated and bleakly beautiful place for a solitary [person] to live in prayer and meditation on the western fringes of northern Europe, remains powerful through centuries of literary and popular accounts of these places.[11]

Vikings in the Arctic

Unfortunately for the Irish monks who settled in Iceland, their solitude lasted only a couple of centuries. In the last few decades of the ninth century (the 800s), seemingly out of nowhere appeared the hardy, at times fierce Scandinavian people known as the Vikings (or Norse, or Northmen). Originating in what are now Denmark, Norway, and Sweden, the Vikings exploded outward from their homelands in the 700s and 800s. Some were raiders who attacked and looted the coasts of England, Ireland, France, and other European lands. Others were explorers and settlers who sought new areas to raise their children and livestock.

Members of this second breed of Vikings landed in Iceland. They rapidly drove away the Irish residents and by 930 had taken possession of almost all of the island's grazing lands, most of which were located near the coasts. Not long after that, the number of Norse in Iceland reached at least thirty thousand. Once again, population growth stimulated the desire for expansion, and the next major target for settlement was Greenland. Lying a few hundred miles west of Iceland, Greenland is a huge and mostly cold and desolate island, large portions of which are located above the Arctic Circle.

The initial Viking settlement of Greenland was spearheaded by Erik the Red, a strong leader and colorful character who was born in Norway and later made a home in Iceland. In the 980s he and his companions established two colonies.

The first was on Greenland's southeastern coast; the other was located about 300 miles (483km) up its western coast. The two outposts swiftly attained a combined population of some three thousand. To support themselves, in addition to raising sheep and cattle they grew grains, hunted polar bears and walruses, and traded with tribes of Inuit who lived on various nearby Arctic islands.

Evidence suggests that once the colonies in southern Greenland were well-established, some Viking explorers sailed northward along the island's long, winding coast. In doing so, their intent was not to reach the North Pole, which they had no idea existed, but to seek out new areas for settlement. In most cases, they saw that said regions, now known to be well north of the Arctic Circle, were too cold and inhospitable for settlement. But in visiting them they did learn that huge ice sheets, icebergs, and vast frozen landscapes existed not far north of the areas in which they did settle.

A well-documented example of this early polar exploration is recounted in one of the many Viking sagas, long written narratives telling of the adventures of notable Norse men and women. It tells of the exploits of one of Erik the Red's friends, Thorgisl, who initially dwelled in Iceland. In about 990 Erik invited him to come and live in the western Greenland colony, and roughly seven years later Thorgisl gathered his family and made the trip.

The story of the fateful voyage was later recorded by Icelandic Christian priests. Driven off course by bad weather, Thorgisl ended up in Baffin Bay, the wide channel that separates Baffin Island and Greenland. In this way, he became the first-known European to inspect the bay, which later explorers would use as a major gateway to the North Pole. The following excerpt from Thorgisl's saga describes some of the difficulties he and his companions encountered after becoming lost.

Erik the Red is credited with establishing the first Viking settlement on Greenland in the A.D. 980s.

First, their ship broke up, and then they found themselves trapped because the local bays were choked by long-lasting ice packs:

> One evening they wrecked their ship on the ice mountains [lining Baffin Bay] on a sand bank in a certain fiord [long, narrow, cliff-lined inlet]. The ship broke up and the stern drifted ashore to the south of where they were. All the people and livestock were saved. . . . It was then early in October, a week before winter began. Glaciers ran around the sides of the bay and the most habitable spot lay in the western part of it.[12]

Not the Last

Although Erik and Thorgisl seem to have been the first Viking Arctic explorers, they were not the last. Surviving writings indicate that in 1266 the western Greenland colony launched an expedition to find the homeland (if any) of some Inuit who had been recently threatening the colony. The ultimate outcome of the mission is unknown. But it appears that the Norse party reached the northernmost coasts of Baffin Bay. Viking travelers also attained northern Greenland, as evidenced by the modern discovery of a Norse artifact on the island at latitude 73° north, a full seven degrees above the Arctic Circle. In addition, modern explorers found evidence that Viking hunters frequented Ellesmere Island at a latitude of more than

79° north, only a few hundred miles below the North Pole.

These expeditions plied the icy regions northwest of Europe. Meanwhile, other Vikings were exploring the areas lying due north and northeast of Scandinavia. The best-known example was a Norwegian Viking trader named Ottar (or Ohthere). In an account he wrote himself, he describes a journey he undertook in about 860 far to the north of his homeland. Modern scholars think he reached the Barents Sea, bordering what is now northern Finland, perhaps making it six or more degrees north of the Arctic Circle. His narrative reads in part:

> [I] was determined to find out [how] far this country extended northward, or whether any one lived to the north of the [icy] waste[lands]. With this intent [I] proceeded northward along the coast, leaving all the way the wasteland on the starboard, and the wide sea on the backboard, for three days. [I] was then as far north as the whale-hunters ever go. . . . All the land to [my] right during [my] whole voyage was uncultivated and without inhabitants, except a few fishermen, fowlers, and hunters, all of whom were Finlanders; and [I] had nothing but the wide sea on [my] left all the way.[13]

Ottar's mention of Finnish hunters in the far north is revealing. Surviving ancient and medieval written accounts

Trapped by Ice and Bad Weather

In this excerpt from the Viking Thorgisl's saga, after being shipwrecked off the coast of Green-land, he and his men erect a large shelter and build a new boat. But they still find themselves trapped by ice and inclement weather.

Here they all labored to build a hall [house] which they divided into two parts with a cross partition [wall]. Thorgisl's party had one end of the hall and [his friend] Iostan's party the other. They had saved a little meal from the wreck and some other [supplies], and the two parties shared these things. Most of their surviving cattle died. . . . Early in the winter both parties had been working at rebuilding their ship. Now Thorgisl and his men completed a new one out of the wreckage. But they could not get away that summer because the fiord ice did not clear out of the bay. They spent the summer hunting and building up their stocks of provisions. The next winter began [and] when the second spring arrived they still could not get away.

Quoted in Farley Mowat, *The Polar Passion: The Quest for the North Pole, with Selections from the Artic Journals.* Boston: Little, Brown, 1967, pp. 21–22.

After being shipwrecked off the coast of Greenland, Thorgisl's Vikings built a new boat but remained in the grip of enormous ice floes.

of explorers almost always describe those who either purposely set out to find something or who were shipwrecked or lost. Little or no mention is made of local hunters and fishermen, whose names and personal stories no one will ever know. Trying to feed their families and villages, they often ranged hundreds of miles from home, braving the dangers of the desolate, freezing regions far north of the Arctic Circle. The Finns seen by Ottar and the Viking hunters on Ellesmere Island are only two examples. Archaeological evidence points to another—hunters and fishermen from England, who were casting their nets in the frigid waters around Greenland at least by the early 1400s. These obscure but valiant individuals had no way of knowing that they were the unsung forbears of later heroic polar explorers who would gain fame and glory for their headlong, often reckless attempts to reach the top of the world.

Chapter Two

Quests for the Northern Passages

In the centuries when Irish Monks, Viking settlers, and enterprising hunters and fishermen frequented Arctic waters and islands, no general vision of or plan for the polar region existed. These various parties explored and exploited the frozen northern wildernesses more or less randomly and as need dictated. This situation changed after the year 1492, the year that Christopher Columbus, an Italian mariner sailing for Spain, landed in the West Indies, now the Caribbean Sea.

An important fact to note is that Columbus was attempting to reach the East Indies and Cathay (the name then used for China) by sailing west from Europe. Those places in the Far East held the promise of vast riches and natural resources that Europe might exploit through trade and other means. Columbus had no idea that a vast new continent (actually two, North and South America), bordered by two wide oceans, lay between Europe and China. When this fact was confirmed, Europeans still wanted to reach and exploit the Far East. But now they realized they needed to find navigable routes through the newfound continental barriers.

This realization was particularly challenging for England, the Netherlands, and France, among the handful of nations that took the lead in exploring and exploiting the Americas. The problem was that two other leaders—Spain and Portugal—had early and quickly seized possession of most of the central and southern American regions. These included Florida (then encompassing most of the southeastern United States), Mexico, and Brazil. "For the merchants and seamen of other countries," especially the English and Dutch, historian L.P. Kirwan points out, "only the northern routes to Cathay, through the ice and fogs and blizzards of the Arctic, remained."[14]

Of these conjectured northern routes to the Pacific, one was assumed to run past Greenland, into the Arctic Ocean, and along or through the coasts of what is now northern Canada. Appropriately, it came to be called the Northwest Passage. The other main northern route that Europeans speculated might lead to the Far East was thought to run in the opposite direction. Supposedly this so-called Northeast Passage ran along the northern coasts of Scandinavia, Russia, and Siberia and then entered the Pacific near northern China and Japan.

Efforts to find one or both of these routes became large-scale, sometimes desperate national enterprises. They consumed vast amounts of time, money, and resources and cost the lives of numerous explorers and sailors. According to one modern expert:

The campaign to reach the luxurious profusion [material abundance] of the Pacific [region] by sailing along the north coast of North America or across the top of Siberia was fought relentlessly for

This satellite photo shows the Northwest Passage between Greenland and Canada. People incorrectly conjectured that it would lead to China.

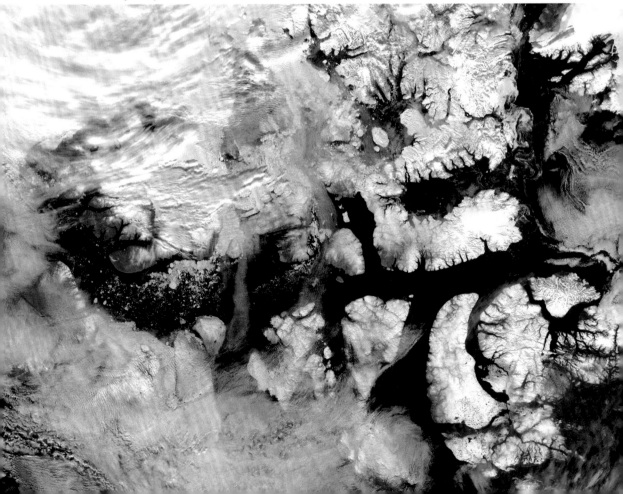

the next three hundred years. The Search for a Northeast or Northwest Passage was a remarkable triumph of greed over experience, and it killed thousands of strong and healthy young men in slow and messy ways without achieving anything more lucrative than better cartography [map-making].[15]

Cathay Closer than Thought?

While Spain and Portugal poured vast sums of money into settling and exploiting Central and South America, England and the Netherlands took an early lead in exploring the regions situated from New England northward, including the lands lying above the Arctic Circle. At first, concerns for establishing long-term settlements in these areas were minimal. Instead, leading English and Dutch politicians and merchants focused most of their attention on searching for the Northwest Passage.

Among the first major expeditions to attempt this arduous task was that of England's Martin Frobisher, who departed with three ships in 1576. Like other explorers of his era, he employed small wooden sailing ships featuring one or two main masts. Such a vessel carried primitive guns and other weapons for hunting and defense; some small rowboats and fishing gear; cheap beads and other trinkets for trade with any natives that might be encountered; and enough food and water for several weeks. (The assumption was that the crew would find more food and water in the lands they visited.) Frobisher first reached southern Greenland, and from there crossed Baffin Bay and landed on the southern end of Baffin Island. Soon afterward, not far south of the Arctic Circle, he found the mouth of a wide channel winding westward through the island. It later became known as Frobisher Bay. For unknown reasons, Frobisher did not continue to explore the bay, but he was sure he had found the Northwest Passage. Later explorers showed that the waterway was only a wide inlet that dead-ended farther inland.

Frobisher was astounded when he was greeted by a sort of welcoming party in the form of dozens of Inuit in canoes, perhaps hoping to trade with the strangers. He noted their somewhat Mongoloid features and from that surmised that they were Asian. That appears to have led him to believe that Cathay must lie closer than most people had thought— perhaps only a few hundred miles farther west. Hoping to prove that theory to people back in England, he forcefully yanked one of the natives from a canoe and kept him as a hostage. (The captive, whom many English came to call the "Strange Man of Cathay," died shortly after reaching England.)

In another highlight of the expedition, a powerful storm struck Frobisher's ship, the *Gabriel*, which almost sank. In fact, his crew survived mainly through his courage, quick thinking, and physical dexterity. Mountainous waves and powerful wind gusts caused the vessel to heel over, after which water gushed

Why England Sought the Northwest Passage

Early in the great age of European exploration, noted English navigator Richard Chancellor explained why leading Englishmen had concluded that finding a northern route through the Americas to Cathay (China) was crucial:

A t the time, our merchants perceived the commodities and wares of England to be in small request with the countries and people about us, [and] that those merchandises which strangers in the time and memory of our ancestors did earnestly seek and desire were now neglected [and] all foreign merchandises in great account and their prices wonderfully raised. [The] citizens of London and men of great wisdom . . . began to think [how] this mischief might be remedied. . . . Seeing that the wealth of the Spaniards and Portuguese by the discovery and search of new trade [routes] and countries were marvelously increased . . . they [the English] thereupon resolved [to do the same and search for] a new and strange navigation [i.e., the Northwest Passage].

Quoted in L.P. Kirwin, *A History of Polar Exploration.* New York: Norton, 1960, p. 15.

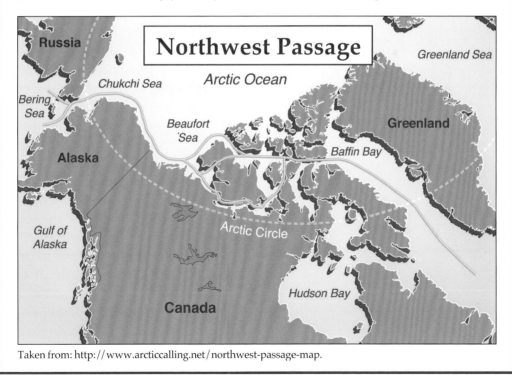

Taken from: http://www.arcticcalling.net/northwest-passage-map.

into it. "She lay still," a contemporary account of the expedition states. "In this distress, when all the men in the ship had lost their courage, and did despair of life, the captain, like himself, with valiant courage, stood up and passed along the ship's side in the chain wales [wooden planks running horizontally along the vessel's outer edge] lying on her flat side."[16] After this incredible display of strength and agility, Frobisher produced a knife and cut away the mizzen sail, reducing the force of the wind on the ship and thereby allowing it to slowly regain its upright position.

England's Martin Frobisher made one of the first voyages in search of the Northwest Passage.

For a while, it seemed as though Frobisher might become as much a hero with his queen, Elizabeth I, and the English people as he had with his own men. During the trip he found some black rocks that he and his advisers thought was an exotic form of gold. On returning to England, the queen and her own advisers accepted that it was indeed gold. Temporarily setting aside the quest for the Northwest Passage, the government funded a new Frobisher expedition with the goal of bringing home as much of the precious ore as possible. Unfortunately for all involved, the substance turned out to be worthless rock rather than gold. Frobisher was discredited and his claims to have found a quick route to Cathay were summarily dismissed.

Davis and Barents

The next Englishman to take up the challenge of finding the Northwest Passage was an experienced sailor named John Davis. In 1585 he landed in Greenland and proceeded to accurately map its western coast, a feat that significantly aided later explorers in the region. Davis also crossed over the Arctic Circle and then entered Cumberland Sound, a wide inlet of Baffin Island lying north of Frobisher Bay. Davis hoped the sound was the entrance to the Northwest Passage but did not take the time to prove it by exploring its full length. Instead, he spent much of his time collecting new scientific data along the coasts of Greenland and Baffin Island. Making a vocabulary of the Inuit language was only one of his many projects. About

Battle with a Bear

During his search for the Northeast Passage, Willem Barents and his men encountered a polar bear, which they viewed as an exotic creature. A hunt ensued, which Barents describes in his writings:

Being so well furnished of men and weapons, we rowed with our boats unto the bear and fought with her [for about two hours], for our weapons could do her little hurt. And amongst the blows that we gave her, one of our men struck her into the back with an axe which struck fast [got stuck] in her, and yet she swam away with it. But we rowed after her, and at last we cut her head in sunder with an axe, wherewith [at which point] she died.

Quoted in David Mountfield, *A History of Polar Exploration*. New York: Dial, 1976, p. 37.

An engraving created after the voyage of Willem Barents depicts the Barents party's encounter with a polar bear.

Davis's dedication to science and the expansion of human knowledge, scholar David Mountfield remarks:

> Much more than Frobisher, he was moved by the spirit of scientific curiosity and was interested in everything he saw. He never anchored in a [bay or other waterway] without attempting to explore the hinterland [general vicinity], investigate the flora and fauna, and make contact with the inhabitants.[17]

Because he took the time to record so much of what he encountered, Davis also significantly aided later explorers of the Arctic region. His nineteenth-century biographer, Clements R. Markham, admiringly sums up Davis's accomplishments, saying that he

> converted the Arctic regions from a confused myth into a defined area, the physical aspects and conditions of which were understood as far as they were known. He not only described and mapped the extensive tract explored by himself, but he clearly pointed out the work cut out for his successors. . . . His true-hearted devotion to the cause of Arctic discovery, his patient scientific research, his loyalty to his employers, his dauntless gallantry and enthusiasm, form an example which will be a beacon-light to maritime explorers for all time to come.[18]

In 1588, while Davis was still hard at work, England and Spain went to war. Threatened by the famous Spanish Armada (a huge war fleet), the English needed all of their experienced naval officers. So Davis had to put a temporary hold on his explorations.

During this lull, the Dutch stepped in, initially with a skilled navigator named Willem Barents, who set out to find the Northeast Passage. (Barents served as navigator and chief adviser under a series of ship captains, and because he was the key figure in each of their expeditions, his name is remembered more than theirs.) Barents reasoned correctly that traversing the Kara Sea, a stretch of ocean lying north of Russia, would constitute one leg of the northeastern route to the Pacific. The problem was that the passage lying between the northern Russian coast and the islands of Novaya and Zemlya was often choked with ice and impassable.

When Barents approached that passage in 1594, however, he found it and the Kara Sea nearly free of ice. He did not realize that this was a highly unusual occurrence. So when the Dutch government sponsored a second expedition into the same region the following year, he and his shipmates were surprised to find that the ice sheets were back. After returning to Amsterdam in embarrassment, Barents became involved in a third expedition in 1596. This time he advised his captain to sail northward around Novaya and Zemlya in an attempt to circumvent the ice.

This strategy turned out to be a serious miscalculation. Barents's ship got caught in the ice and was partially crushed. In the words of one modern observer, "The ship was finished; that was obvious. Help, and the nearest human being, were a thousand miles away. No European had yet lived through an Arctic winter. The prospect was almost hopeless."[19]

Incredibly, however, most of the men survived. They erected a large shelter on a barren island and managed to get through the winter with a loss of only two of their number. In the spring, when the ice began to break up, the fourteen remaining men climbed into the lifeboats and began a successful journey of hundreds of miles to the Russian mainland and safety. Only three of them, including Barents, died on the way.

When Barents attempted to sail north from Zemlya in order to get around the huge masses of ice, his ship got caught in the frozen floes and was crushed.

Stepping Up to the Challenge

Thus, Davis had failed to find the Northwest Passage, and Barents was unable to locate and chart the Northeast Passage. Nevertheless, their expeditions inspired other explorers to step up to the same difficult challenge. In 1607 an English ship captain named Henry Hudson was hired by the Muscovy Company, a group of well-to-do English merchants, to establish a new trade route to the Far East. The bold plan, one never before attempted, was for Hudson to reach the Pacific by sailing directly over or near the North Pole. That such a thing was even possible was based on the then widely accepted notion that the sea around the pole was free of ice during at least part of each year.

That notion turned out to be wrong. Hudson found that the Arctic Ocean was largely filled with a massive polar ice pack that shifted in size and shape each year but that never totally receded. Before turning back, he made it to the Spitzbergen Islands, lying northeast of Greenland. He also found Jan Mayen Island, which Brendan and his monks may have reached centuries before.

In 1608 Hudson set out again to find the Northeast Passage, but his crew mutinied, forcing him to return to England. He launched a third expedition the following year. Hired by the Dutch East India Company, he sailed to North America and explored southern New York, finding the famous river named for him.

Hudson's fourth voyage, in 1610, focused on finding the Northwest Passage. He succeeded in entering and charting the huge waterway in northern Canada that became known as Hudson's Bay in his honor. But soon afterward, for reasons that are still unclear, his crew mutinied. Hudson, his teenage son, and five other men were set adrift in a small boat and never heard from again.

During the remainder of the seventeenth century, the English Civil War and other large-scale events in the British Isles absorbed most of the energies and monies that otherwise might have gone into polar expeditions. So for a while England more or less withdrew from the ongoing contest to find a northern route to the Far East. The next century or so saw Britain gain a global empire and become a world power. It created the strongest navy on Earth and the tonnage of British merchant ships grew from 340,000 to 2,477,000 between 1686 and 1815.

While all that was happening, Russia entered the race to find the Northeast Passage, with impressive results. In 1725 Russia's supreme ruler, Czar Peter the Great (born 1672), singled out Vitus Bering, a Danish-born officer then serving in the Russian navy. Peter wanted to expand knowledge about the eastern sector of the vast Russian nation, including Siberia, the frigid, sparsely populated region occupying much of northeastern Asia. So he called on Bering to begin by charting Russia's far northern coasts. The explorer was also charged with finding a passage to the Pacific and

On his fourth voyage to find a northern passage, Henry Hudson's crew mutinied and cast him, his son, and five crew members adrift in an open boat, never to be heard from again.

determining whether Siberia and North America were connected or separated by a stretch of water.

Bering's efforts were spectacularly successful. In 1729 he found a passage to the Pacific Ocean lying between Siberia and Alaska, which came to be known as the Bering Strait. In a second voyage, which began in 1734, he was accompanied by a small army of close to fifteen hundred sailors, soldiers, and scientists, including a geographer and a mathematician. He covered thousands of miles, created dozens of accurate

The Role Played by Whalers

Henry Hudson's expedition did not manage to find the Northwest Passage. But it did succeed in encouraging the increase of European whalers in Arctic waters. Returning home, Hudson described the many whales he had seen in the waters off Spitzbergen Island, in the southern Arctic. Following up on this report, in 1611 a group of rich English merchants sent two ships to the area to open up whaling operations. The expedition was so successful that other companies and nations immediately sent their own whaling ships to join in the competition for whale oil and blubber. By the mid-1700s, at least three hundred European vessels were roaming the seas between Spitzbergen and Greenland. From time to time, the captains of the whaling ships made Arctic discoveries that they told the explorers about, thereby playing an indirect role in polar exploration.

By the mid-1700s hundreds of ships from many different nations and private enterprises were sailing the coasts of Greenland and hunting whales.

charts, and eventually set foot in Alaska before dying on a small island in the Bering Sea in 1741. Scholar Ralph K. Andrist sums up Bering's accomplishments for Russia and for the advance of polar exploration and the sciences, especially geography:

> Bering's achievements are among the most significant in the annals of Arctic exploration, for he cleared up many doubts and fears about the actual geography of Northeast Asia and Northwest America. Also, but more indirectly, he affected the future course of Arctic exploration. For, in the East, as it had been in the West, exploration was the prelude to colonization and trade. Now Russia's expanding imperialism followed the route of her explorers across the Bering Strait and down the North American coast. By the early nineteenth century, when she was firmly established in Alaska . . . Russia had become a threat to the other great colonial powers of the world.[20]

"Knowledge Is Power"

The success of Bering and other Russians in blazing Arctic paths caused considerable worry among British authorities, who feared that they were losing primacy in northern waters. So in the late 1700s and especially the early 1800s Britain launched major new attempts to find a Northwest Passage. Leading British admiral John Barrow, a strong advocate of that goal, stated the official reason for its importance:

> If [these voyages] were merely to be prosecuted for the sake of making a passage from England to China, and no other purpose, their utility might fairly be questioned. But when the acquisition of knowledge is the groundwork of [such exploration, including] the advancement of every branch of science—astronomy, navigation . . . meteorology, [and] magnetism, and to make collections of [plants and animals], the question [is] easily answered in the words . . . "Knowledge is Power."[21]

Unofficially, Britain had an even more compelling reason to search for the Northwest Passage, one mainly concerned with the country's and the empire's reputation, status, and national identity. As scholar Pierre Berton explains, Britain got caught up in the excitement of possibly finding the Northwest Passage and the North Pole itself:

> The Northwest Passage had glamour. [Nobody] gave out handsome prizes for scientific discoveries, but there would be a sultan's ransom for the first man who could thread his way through the Arctic labyrinth [maze]. National honor was at stake. . . . Every Englishman was convinced that the nineteenth century belonged to Britain. It was

inconceivable that a couple of stout ships could not sweep through the Arctic in a single winter to the greater glory of the Empire.[22]

Attaining the passage and the pole turned out to be far more difficult than most British had expected, however. A long series of skilled, well-supplied, and eager British maritime explorers searched for the Northwest Passage in the decades that followed. Among them were John Ross (1818); William E. Parry (1827); Ross's nephew, James Clark Ross (1839–1843), John Franklin (1845), and Robert McClure (1850–1854). But none was able to find and navigate the passage solely by ship. Meanwhile, the North Pole itself remained ever elusive and out of reach.

Eventually Britain, along with most other nations, decided that finding the Northwest Passage was not worth the time, money, and loss of human lives. The passage was traversed by ship later, in the twentieth century. But by that time the reasons for exploration had changed. More and more the explorers were driven by purely scientific motives or by the desire for personal or national prestige. More important, as interest in the Northwest Passage waned, the attention of the great explorers and their backers increasingly shifted southward. The great age of Antarctic expeditions was dawning.

Chapter Three

Search for the Southern Continent

A curious fact is that long before Europeans could prove the existence of a south-polar continent, they were almost certain that it existed. More than two thousand years before the discovery of Antarctica, on which rests the South Pole, the Greek scholar-philosopher Aristotle described it. As one modern expert puts it:

> He argued that just as a habitable zone [i.e., Europe and Asia] existed below the Arctic Pole, so the symmetry and balance implicit in the concept of the Earth as a perfect sphere required equally a habitable zone in the south. In this global scheme, northern and southern habitable zones were pictured as divided by an impenetrable belt of fire, the belt of the torrid [hot] equatorial regions.[23]

Writing in about a.d. 150, the later ancient Greek astronomer, Ptolemy, concurred with Aristotle about the southern continent, as did Cicero, the noted Roman senator and intellectual. They envisioned it not as a frozen wasteland, but rather as a fertile, well-populated region. Many early depictions of that southern land pictured it extending northward, well into Earth's temperate zones. This idea survived into early modern times, when the cryptic continent was often referred to as *Terra Australis Incognita*, or "unknown southern land." At various moments from the 1500s to the 1700s, Australia, New Zealand, southern South America, and numerous Pacific islands were assumed to be the northern portions of the great southern land mass. Not until the eighteenth century were such claims shown to be undeniably false. Moreover, the actual coastline of the real southern continent, Antarctica, was not sighted by humans until 1820.

The principal reason that Antarctica was so hard for early explorers to approach and verify can be summed up in a single three-letter word—ice. According to researcher Anthony Brandt, the huge Antarctic ice pack

can extend hundreds of miles from the edge of the continent in winter and may cover a total area of 20 million square kilometers. Even in summer enough ice remains attached to Antarctica, in some places permanently, that the early explorers could not approach it in their wooden ships [which broke up easily in the ice]. Thus it is that Antarctica was so slow to be discovered, even when men were looking for it.[24]

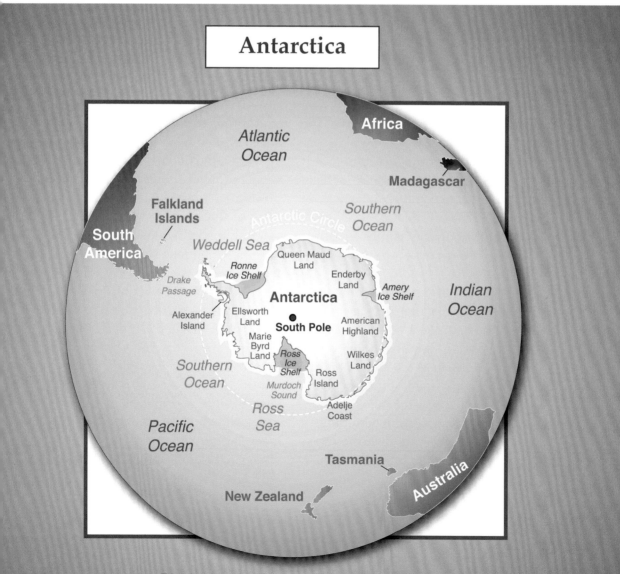

Antarctica

Cicero on the Southern Continent

Among the ancient writers who wrote about the legendary southern continent was the Roman senator, orator, and scholar Marcus Tullius Cicero. In his Scipio's Dream *(part of his larger work* On the Republic, *published in 51 B.C.), he says:*

[T]he] Earth is encircled and encompassed, as it were, by certain zones, of which the two that are most distant from one another and lie . . . toward the vortexes [circular currents] of the heavens in both directions [the poles], are rigid as you see with frost, while the middle of the largest zone [the equator] is burned up with the heat of the sun. Two of these [zones] are habitable. The southern [continent], whose inhabitants imprint their footsteps in an opposite direction to [us], has no relation to [our] race. . . . All that part of the Earth which is inhabited by [us], which narrows toward the south and north, but widens from east to west, is no other than a little island surrounded by that sea which on Earth [we] call the Atlantic.

Quoted in Moses Hadas, ed., *The Basic Works of Cicero*. New York: Modern Library, 1951, p. 166.

Farther South than Supposed?

Europeans were indeed looking for *Terra Australis* from the very start of the great age of exploration that began in the late 1400s. In 1487 Portuguese mariner Bartholomew Diaz rounded the Cape of Good Hope in southernmost Africa. That feat did more than help to establish an oceanic trade route linking Europe and the Far East. It also showed that a large stretch of ocean lay directly south of Africa. That demonstrated that Africa was not an extension of the southern continent, which therefore must lie much farther south than many people supposed.

More clues to the whereabouts of Antarctica emerged in the decades that

followed. In 1501 Italian merchant and adventurer Amerigo Vespucci became the first European to sail down the eastern coast of South America. Later, he was not sure how far south he had traveled. But he did record in his log that he eventually encountered nights lasting longer than normal. This might indicate that he reached a point only a few hundred miles from the southern continent. He writes:

The nights were very long, for the night we had on the seventh of April lasted fifteen hours, the sun being at the end of [the constellation] Ares. [On the same day] we came in sight of new land, along which we ran for [many miles], and found it all a rocky coast, without any sort of inhabitants.[25]

The exact identity of this coastline Vespucci describes remains a mystery. Many modern experts think it was Patagonia, near South America's southern tip. Others suggest it was one of the several small islands lying farther south and southeast of that continent.

Whether Vespucci thought these lands he sighted were part of the legendary southern continent is unclear. But apparently, Ferdinand Magellan, the Portuguese explorer whose ships sailed around the globe in the early 1520s, thought what he himself had seen was part of *Terra Australis*. The channel he passed through near the tip of South America—called the Strait of Magellan in his honor—was bordered in the south by a large island group that came to be called Tierra del Fuego. Magellan assumed that Tierra del Fuego comprised the northern reaches of Antarctica. He was incorrect. No one yet knew exactly where the southern continent was. Nevertheless, its existence was so widely accepted that in the two centuries that followed, European mapmakers routinely included the rough outlines of a large land mass in the seas south of the equator.

The English and French Head South

Although Portuguese navigators at first dominated exploration of the southern seas, the English and French were not far behind. English authorities became serious about entering the contest to find the southern continent as early as the 1570s. This is evidenced by surviving official government statements, one of which encourages mariners to work toward the discovery of "all and any lands, islands, and countries southwards beyond the equatorial, to where the Pole Antarctic has any elevation above the horizon."[26]

One English explorer who answered this call was the colorful ship captain and sometimes pirate Francis Drake. In 1577 Queen Elizabeth sent him, with six ships, to attack Spanish installations in South America. After sailing down that continent's eastern coast, he made it to the Strait of Magellan in 1578. But by that time he had lost all of his vessels except his flagship, the *Pelican* (later renamed the *Golden Hind*). According to Drake's official account, the ship was blown off course and ended up in a wide belt of ocean south of Tierra del Fuego. Accordingly, it became known as the Drake Passage. After that, he sailed northward along South America's western coast, having never found the southern continent. However, he had shown that if such a place did exist, it was not connected to South America. (It should be emphasized that some Spanish and Latin American historians doubt that Drake sailed that far south; they credit the discovery of the so-called Drake Passage to Spanish navigator Francisco de Hoces.)

In a sense, Drake started a trend, as in the decades that followed more and more English and eventually French explorers headed into southern seas. In part, they were motivated by the stirrings of modern science in the 1600s. Scientists became so numerous in England and France that they formed club-like societies in which they met and exchanged ideas. The most prestigious of these groups, England's Royal Society (founded in 1660) and the French Academy of Sciences (1666), also sponsored research and encouraged

Sir Francis Drake circumnavigated the globe in 1577–1580 and was the first English explorer to journey through the southern latitudes during his voyage.

exploration, including expeditions to the polar regions.

Among the English explorers who felt the influence of the new scientific age was Anthony de la Roche. In 1675, piloting his 350-ton (317.5t) ship, the *Hamburg*, he landed on South Georgia, a desolate island lying a few hundred miles north of the Antarctic Circle. That made him the first-known person to set foot on land bordering that latitude.

De la Roche was followed by Edmund Halley, best known for his work in astronomy (including finding the famous comet named for him). Halley sailed the southern seas in 1699–1700 and sighted several huge icebergs, which he thought were small, ice-covered islands. It did not take long to find that these objects posed a serious danger to his ship. They were "milk-white, with perpendicular cliffs all around them," Halley writes in his log.

The great height of them made us conclude them land, but there was no appearance of any tree or green thing on them, but the cliffs as well as the tops were very white. Our people called [one] by the name of Beach Head, which it resembled in form and color, and the [other iceberg was] not less than five miles in [length]. [The next day] the fog was all the morning so thick that we could not see [very far] about us, when on a sudden a mountain of ice began to appear out of the fog about 3 points on our lee bow.

[We managed to dodge it], when another appeared more head-on. . . . This obliged us to tack [veer away] and [we narrowly missed crashing into it].[27]

Giant, treacherous icebergs were also closely observed by French explorer Jean-Baptiste Bouvet de Lozier when he went on a quest for the southern continent in 1739. "We saw some of these islands of ice so high," he writes, "that we could observe them [many miles] off." Bouvet also saw a large ice pack, seemingly the source of the ice islands, and large numbers of penguins and seals. He rightly interpreted all of these as signs "of land being near us."[28] However, the vast ice sheets kept him from finding the still elusive southern continent.

The Perfect Man for the Job

The information about the far side of the world brought back by these English and French explorers was eagerly absorbed by the public and especially the scholarly community. Not surprisingly, a constant call arose for new expeditions to make fresh discoveries and bring back still more data. This intellectual enthusiasm culminated in the most ambitious southern voyages yet attempted. Sponsored by the Royal Society, they were headed by James Cook. He was both an officer in the British navy and a member of the Royal Society, so all agreed that he was the perfect man for the job. "He went to sea while still in his teens," Brandt writes.

British captain and Royal Society member James Cook's explorations demonstrated that if a southern continent did exist it was a lot farther south than previously thought.

He rose rapidly [through the naval ranks], displaying considerable ability both as a navigator and a chart-maker. The charts he made of the St. Lawrence River [in Canada] in the late 1750s were used for a hundred years. [He] was not only skillful, he was also a careful observer and precise in his descriptions. He proved to be adept with native populations. . . . He was cool under pressure and he was tolerant. People regard him still as perhaps the greatest explorer of all time.[29]

On his first voyage, lasting from 1768 to 1771, Cook first disposed of the still often proposed idea that *Terra Australis* projected northward into the Pacific Ocean. He landed in Tahiti, went on to circumnavigate and chart the coasts of New Zealand, and also made it to the eastern coasts of Australia. The journey demonstrated conclusively that the southern continent, if it did exist, must lie much farther south than any explorer had yet ventured.

Hoping to be the first to so venture, Cook left on his second voyage in 1772. His two well-stocked ships, the *Resolution* and the *Adventure*, carried a full staff of skilled scientists and other experts. Among others, they included an astronomer, botanist, naturalist (a

Nothing but Ice

On January 18, 1773, James Cook and his men first encountered the vast fields of ice surrounding much of Antarctica, as he describes it in his journal:

At 4 o'Clock we discovered from the mast-head thirty-eight islands of ice extending from the one bow to the other, that is from the SE to West, and soon afterward we discovered field or packed ice in the same direction and had so many loose pieces about the ship that we were obliged to look for one and bear up for another, the number increased so fast upon us that at ¾ past six . . . the ice was so thick and close that we could proceed no further, but were fain [reluctant] to tack and stand from [avoid] it. From the mast-head I could see nothing to the southward but ice.

Quoted in Walker Chapman, ed., *Antarctic Conquest: The Great Explorers in Their Own Words*. New York: Bobbs-Merrill, 1965, pp. 27–28.

James Cook's Resolution *maneuvers through the Antarctic pack ice as* Adventure *stands back in the distance in January 1773.*

sort of combination biologist and bota-nist), and two expert landscape artists (because photography had not yet been invented).

Swiftly moving southward to the low-est reaches of the Atlantic, the expedi-tion sighted its first large icebergs in December 1772. Soon afterward, on Jan-uary 17, 1773, the ships became the first in history to cross the Antarctic Circle. Eventually, after sailing for months and crossing the Antarctic Circle two more times, Cook found that the pack ice was too dense to allow any more progress. He had no choice, therefore, but to turn back.

What Cook did not realize at the time was that he and his men had come with-in a mere 75 miles (121km) of the coast of Antarctica. But though he never saw the continent that he sometimes called the "Grand Object," he was sure it was there, floating agonizingly just out of reach. Earlier, he had recorded in his log: "It is a general received opinion that ice is formed near land. If so, then there must be land in the neighborhood of this ice."[30] Later, on January 30, 1774, just before turning back, he followed up on that same theme as well as expressed his feelings about his inability to press onward:

It was indeed my opinion, as well as the opinion of most on board, that this [pack] ice extended quite to the Pole or perhaps joins to some land [not far from here], where all the ice[bergs we have seen] are first formed and afterwards broke off

[and were] brought to the north by the currents. . . . As we drew near this ice some penguins were heard [and] indeed, if there was any land behind this ice, it could afford no better retreat for birds or any other animals, than the ice itself. . . . I, who had ambition not only to go farther than anyone had done before, but as far as it was possible for man to go, was not sorry with meeting with this [obstacle], as it in some measure . . . shortened the dangers and hardships [we would likely have met in navigating] the southern polar regions.[31]

Antarctica Finally Sighted

For half a century Cook's milestone in southern exploration remained untouched, as no one attempted to sail farther south than he had. In time, how-ever, the same demands for extending the boundaries of knowledge that had challenged him came to entice others to go farther. In the early nineteenth cen-tury, a race developed among the major industrialized nations to be first to sight the mystifying southern continent.

The result was that three explorers from three separate countries saw that continent in the same year, and each claimed priority over the others. One of them, Edward Bransfield, a captain in the British navy, crossed the Antarctic Circle, and on January 30, 1820, sight-ed a chain of frozen islands up ahead. "The whole of these," he wrote, "formed a prospect [vista] the most gloomy that

A Desert of Ice

Some experts have compared Antarctica to a desert because, despite its huge fields of ice and snow, it receives only minimal rainfall each year. According to National Geographic Society scholar Anthony Brandt:

[A]ntarctica] is some two-thirds the size of North America and only 4 percent of its surface area is free of ice. . . . That ice contains 40 percent of the world's fresh water, yet Antarctica has the annual precipitation of a desert. It is in fact the driest continent of the world's seven. Such is the persistence of life, that lichens and mosses do grow on that 4 percent of surface that is not covered by ice, and these few dry valleys, as they are known, and the other dry areas, also contain one species of spider and some insects. But otherwise, Antarctica is dead. The only larger life forms found [there] are found in the surrounding ocean.

Anthony Brandt, ed., *The South Pole: A Historical Reader*. Washington, DC: National Geographic, 2004, p. x.

Lichen and moss grow beneath Blue Glacier in Antarctica. They are found on the 4 percent of Antarctica's surface not covered by ice.

can be imagined, and the only cheer that sight afforded us was the idea that this might be the long-sought southern continent, as land was undoubtedly seen."[32] An English naval surgeon on board Bransfield's ship added:

> The whole line of coast appeared high, bold, and rugged. [It rose] abruptly from the sea in perpendicular [vertical] snowy cliffs, except here and there where the naked face of a barren black rock showed itself amongst them. In the interior, the land . . . sloped gradually and gently upwards into high hills.[33]

The second claimant was an American seaman from Connecticut, Nathaniel Palmer. On November 20, 1820, he also saw the Antarctic coast, with mountains rising in the distance. According to a writer who interviewed him:

> He found it to be an extensive, mountainous country, more sterile and dismal if possible, and more heavily loaded with ice and snow, than the [islands off the coast]. . . . The main part of the coast was icebound, although [it was] midsummer in this hemisphere, and a landing consequently difficult.[34]

A Russian naval officer, Fabian von Bellingshausen, most likely beat both Bransfield and Palmer to the continent. He brought two ships—the *Vostok* and *Mirny*—within the Antarctic Circle. On January 28, 1820, he reached a point about 20 miles (32km) from the continent's rugged coast. He later described a snow-covered mainland that "sloped upwards towards the south to a distance so far [away] that its end was out of sight."[35]

For a long time, it appeared that Bransfield had been first to see the southern continent. In large part this was because Bellinghausen's log was not translated into English until the twentieth century and remained obscure in the West. Today, however, most scholars accept that the Russian explorer beat Bransfield by two days.

None of these pioneers actually set foot on Antarctica, however. The first person to do so was another Connecticut sailor, seal-hunter John Davis. He and his men claimed they came ashore on the Antarctic coast on February 7, 1821. It would be a long time, however, before humans reached the South Pole, which is situated hundreds of miles farther inland over unbelievably inhospitable and dangerous ground. Thus, the race to find the fabled *Terra Australis* was finally over; but the competition to set foot on the southern pole had just begun.

Chapter Four

The Contest for the North Pole

After most nations and explorers more or less gave up on finding the Northwest Passage in the mid-1800s, the focus of polar exploration shifted more toward the south and the Antarctic. However, by 1890 interest in the Arctic had revived. This time the goal was to reach the geographical North Pole rather than to find a sea route to the Far East.

To achieve this tremendously difficult goal, the explorers, as before, started out in wooden sailing ships. But with thousands of square miles of pack ice surrounding the pole, ships could go only so far. The men had to disembark and travel much of the way on foot. Indeed, in the days before motorized forms of transport, the final, crucial approaches to both poles were made on foot, sometimes with the aid of sledges (sleds) drawn by dogs. Under such rigorous constraints, the polar explorers of the late 1800s and early 1900s were attempt-ing to overcome nature's full fury almost solely with their strength, endurance, wits, and courage.

Because all gear and supplies had to be carried, usually on the sledges, the amount that could be taken was limited. The design of the sledges themselves was often based on the versions used for centuries by the Inuit. Typically they were 6 feet to 9 feet (1.8m to 2.7m) long, with ski-like runners on the bottom and sometimes a canvas sail to catch the wind and give a little extra push. The standard gear carried in the sledges included tents that could be sealed off from the elements; warm sleeping bags and tunics, often made of reindeer fur; woolen underwear and sweaters; goggles with lenses of smoked glass to cut down the glare of the sun reflecting off ice and snow; tin flasks for drinking melted snow; a portable cooking stove; and instruments, including compass and sextant, to help determine location.

Arctic Explorers' Routes

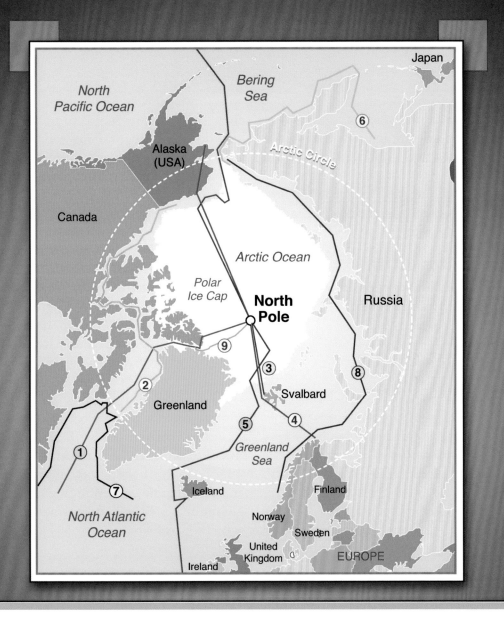

1. **Robert Peary, 1909**
2. Roald Amundsen, 1905
3. Richard Byrd, 1926
4. Amundsen, Lincoln Ellsworth, Nobile, 1926
5. **USS *Nautilus*, 1958**
6. Vitus Bering, 1725–28
7. **John Davis, 1585**
8. **Otto Nordenskiold, 1878–79**
9. Frederick Cook, 1908

That the polar explorers took such huge risks with so few materials to back them up says much about their personalities and how the social outlooks of their time shaped their mental attitudes. As Moss puts it:

All of those who wanted to be first at the North and South Poles wanted personal fame and national heroism, and the governments that funded them wanted enhanced prestige for their nation-states, but nobody expected any concrete or tangible benefits of any description to result from "bagging" a pole. It was an exercise in mathematics and public relations that seemed to have little to do with the starvation and frostbite [endured by many of the explorers].[36]

Frederick Cook's Early Exploits

The contest to be first to reach the North Pole was just such a grand exercise in public relations. It also developed into a very real and at times fierce rivalry among the various explorers who committed themselves to this goal. Particularly controversial was the competition between two American explorers—Robert Peary and Frederick Cook. They engaged in a spirited battle to beat each other to the pole. Moreover, in the years following their expeditions each claimed victory and tried to discredit the other in the eyes of the public and scientific community. The irony is that, in the end, to nearly everyone's surprise, both men were discredit-

ed, and the priority for reaching the North Pole went to a third party.

Another unusual twist to the story is that Cook and Peary started off as friends. Cook, who grew up in poverty in a small town in New York State, worked his way through medical school in New York City and received his doctor of medicine, or MD, degree in 1890. Born in Pennsylvania, Peary attended Bowdoin College in Maine and became a civil engineer and naval officer. When Peary was planning to explore northern Greenland in 1891, he placed an ad in the newspaper for a surgeon for the expedition. Cook answered the ad and accompanied Peary to Greenland.

As it turned out, Cook was just as ambitious and driven as Peary and desired to lead his own Arctic expeditions. So in 1894 Cook managed to obtain financing for his own Greenland venture, which now made him Peary's rival. Cook's trip to Greenland that year did not accomplish much beyond helping to establish him as a bona fide polar explorer. It soon paid off, as he was asked to serve as the surgeon of a large 1897 Belgian Antarctic expedition. During that trip he earned high praise for saving many lives and became friends with the great Norwegian polar explorer Roald Amundsen.

The Stepping-Stones to Success

The rivalry between Cook and Peary began to intensify soon after the turn of the century, when the latter was trying to conquer the North Pole. Cook wanted

Cook's Fictitious Recollection

In this excerpt from his diary, Frederick Cook describes reaching the North Pole, although the feat was later proved to be fabricated.

We were excited to fever heat. Even the dogs caught the infection. They rushed along at a pace which made it difficult for me to keep a sufficient advance to set a good course. . . . The same expanse of moving seas of ice on which we had gazed for 500 miles swam about us as we drove onward. [We] were all lifted to the paradise of winners as we stepped over the snows of a destiny for which we had risked life and suffered the fortunes of hell. Constantly I watched my instruments in recording this final reach. Nearer and nearer they recorded our approach. At last we touched the mark! We were at the top of the world! The flag is flung to the frigid breezes of the North Pole! . . . With my two [Inuit] companions I could not converse fully, [so] I was alone. I was victorious. But how desolate, how dreadful was the victory. About us was no life, nothing to relieve the monotony of frost and a dead world of ice. A wild eagerness to get back to land seized me.

Quoted in Farley Mowat, *The Polar Passion: The Quest for the North Pole, with Selections from the Arctic Journals.* Boston: Little, Brown, 1967, pp. 264–65.

A portrait of Dr. Frederick Cook in 1930. His claims of reaching the North Pole were later proved unfounded.

Le Petit Journal

ADMINISTRATION
61, RUE LAFAYETTE, 61

Les manuscrits ne sont pas rendus

On s'abonne sans frais
dans tous les bureaux de poste

5 CENT. SUPPLÉMENT ILLUSTRÉ 5 CENT.

20me Année ** Numéro 987
DIMANCHE 19 SEPTEMBRE 1909

ABONNEMENTS

SIX MOIS UN AN
SEINE et SEINE-ET-OISE.. 2 fr. 3 fr. 50
DÉPARTEMENTS............ 2 fr. 4 fr. »
ÉTRANGER .... 2 50 5 fr. »

LA CONQUÊTE DU POLE NORD
Le docteur Cook et le commandant Peary s'en disputent la gloire

The French magazine Le Petit Journal's *story lampooned the rivalry between Peary and Cook.*

to be first to the pole, too. But he had neither the money nor the wealthy connections required to mount an expedition of that size. So he concocted a daring plan, summarized by Brandt:

> He needed a dramatic achievement to attract patrons and the idea for it came from an article in *National Geographic* about Mt. McKinley in Alaska, the highest mountain in North America. No one had climbed it yet. If he could be the first up the mountain, Cook reasoned, money for a North Pole expedition would be easy to find.[37]

Cook made his first attempt to scale Mt. McKinley in 1903. It was unsuccessful, so he tried again in 1906. The funding for the expedition came from Herschel Parker, a professor at Columbia University. Parker's condition in giving Cook the money was that he be allowed to go along, and soon a third man, a recent Harvard graduate named Belmore Browne, joined them. The three looked for promising routes up the steep and dangerous peak but found none. So they split up. Cook said he planned to keep looking for a way up on his own, and when Browne offered to go along, Cook told him no. A couple of months later, Cook came walking out of Mt. McKinley's foothills, claiming he had

indeed found a route and made it to the summit as well.

Later, as it turned out, a number of people would challenge Cook, saying that he never actually climbed to the mountain's top. But for the time being, most people accepted his claim. This cemented his reputation as a daring explorer and risk taker and helped him raise money to finance his own mission to the North Pole.

Indeed, Cook managed to get the money he needed quickly. In preparation for the trip to the pole, he spent the winter of 1907 in a remote Inuit camp in northern Greenland. In February 1908 he departed with nine Inuit and crossed to Axel Heiberg Island (situated northwest of Ellesmere Island). Then, on March 18, taking two of the Inuit with him along with two sledges and twenty-eight dogs, he headed due north over the pack ice. As one modern observer points out, "Neither of the two men he took with him could speak English, and neither of them knew a sextant from a thermometer. [So] the question of whether he reached the Pole or not would depend entirely on Cook's own testimony."[38]

In his expedition log, Cook uses colorful prose to describe the thrill of skirting across the ice toward his goal—the top of the world:

> Bounding joyously forward, with a stimulated mind, I reviewed the journey. Obstacle after obstacle had been overcome. Each battle won gave a spiritual thrill and courage to scale the next barrier. Thus

had been ever, and was still, in the unequal struggles between human and inanimate nature, an incentive to go onward, ever onward, up the stepping-stones to ultimate success. And now, after a life-denying struggle in a world where every element of nature is against the life and progress of man, triumph came with steadily measured reaches of fifteen miles a day.[39]

Cook later said that he arrived at the North Pole on April 21, 1908. According to his account, he spent twenty-four hours there and then headed back toward Greenland. It appeared that, in reaching the North Pole and living to tell about it, he had shattered one of the greatest remaining natural barriers on Earth.

Peary's Approach to Conquest

Soon, however, a series of events began to cast doubt on Cook's declaration that he had reached the pole first. It began with a claim to polar priority made by Peary within the same year that Cook made his own claim. Peary had set out

African American explorer Matthew Henson, left, forged an early friendship with Robert Peary, right, on numerous Arctic expeditions.

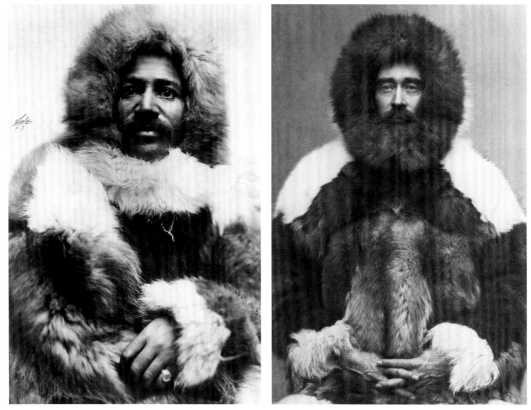

A Tribute to Himself

On his way back from his attempt to reach the North Pole, Robert Peary penned a tribute to himself in his diary, saying:

My life['s] work is accomplished. The thing which it was intended from the beginning that I should do, the thing which I believed could be done, and that I could do, I have done. I have got the North Pole out of my system after twenty-three years of effort, hard work, disappointments, hardships, privations . . . suffering, and some risks. I have won the last great geographical prize, the North Pole, for the credit of the United States. This work is the finish, the cap and climax of nearly four hundred years of effort, loss of life, and expenditures of fortunes by the civilized nations of the world, and it has been accomplished in a way that is thoroughly American. I am content.

Quoted in Fergus Fleming, *Ninety Degrees North: The Quest for the North Pole.* New York: Grove, 2001, pp. 367–68.

for the North Pole in July 1908, about four months after Cook had departed for the same destination. Moreover, Peary was still on his return journey from the Arctic in 1909 when Cook got back and made his public announcement about reaching the pole.

Peary's approach to conquering the pole was somewhat different than Cook's. Like Cook, Peary was strongly preoccupied with enhancing his own reputation. But Peary also had what those who knew him called a fanatical attraction to the pole itself and to being the first human to stand atop it. "His obsession with the Pole" haunted him and "took him over," according to one authority. "It made him imperious

[arrogant], driven, [and] unpleasant to be around."[40]

Thus, in Peary's view nearly everything he did, including all of his earlier expeditions, constituted preparations for accomplishing his life's dream—reaching the North Pole. His several Greenland expeditions in the 1890s, for instance, were intended to teach him how to survive on long treks through ice-covered wilderness. They were also designed to make him a famous explorer. In this, they succeeded, for during his 1892 trip he showed the scientific world, for the first time, that Greenland was definitely an island and not part of one of the major continents.

It was during these early Arctic journeys that Peary forged a close relationship with Matthew Henson. Born in Maryland in 1866, Henson was the only African American explorer in that era of polar discovery. At age twelve he had served as a cabin boy on a merchant ship and later had worked his way up through the ranks to become a skilled navigator. Henson met Peary in 1887, and the two became constant companions on numerous later expeditions.

Henson was with his mentor in 1898 when Peary first tried to reach the pole. While still in northern Greenland, Peary encountered a bout of unusually severe cold that caused his toes to become badly frostbitten. Eight of them had to be amputated. He was so obsessed with achieving his goal, he famously quipped, "A few toes aren't much to give to achieve the Pole."[41] Eventually he was able to continue, now walking with a marked limp, and only when the pack ice began drifting the wrong way was he forced to turn back.

"MINE at Last"

Incredibly, Peary was still not beaten. By 1908 he mounted his biggest Arctic polar expedition yet—consisting of nineteen sledges, 133 dogs, and twenty-four men. Of these men, five—Henson and four Inuit—accompanied him on the final leg of the trip. In his log Peary recorded reaching his ultimate goal on April 6, 1909. "The Pole at last!!!" he scribbled in his diary. "The prize of 3 centuries, my dream and ambition for 23 years, mine at last. I cannot bring myself to realize it."[42]

He also recorded how he left behind a token of his presence:

I deposited a glass bottle containing a diagonal strip of my flag and records [including] "90 N. Lat., North Pole, April 6, 1909. Arrived here today. . . . The expedition under my command, which has succeeded in reaching the Pole, [has done so] for the purpose of securing the geographical prize, if possible, for the honor and prestige of the United States of America.[43]

On his return to civilization, Peary announced that he had been the first person to reach the North Pole. To his surprise and ire, he found that his rival, Cook, had already made that same claim. But Peary found a great deal of satisfaction when Cook was soon discredited. One major strike against Cook was the discovery that he had not conquered Mt. McKinley, as he had earlier asserted. Two separate investigations launched in 1910 confirmed that he had lied. One found that a photo supposedly taken atop the 20,000-foot (6,000m) peak had actually been taken on a 5,000-foot (1,500m) mountain 20 miles (32km) away.

Furthermore, Cook had presented the documentation of his polar trek to a committee of experts in Copenhagen, Denmark. It included readings he claimed to have taken, using his instruments and the stars, of his changing positions as he moved toward and away from the pole. After studying the materials, the committee members stated: "The documents submitted to us are of such an unsatisfactory character that it is not possible to declare with certainty that the astronomical observations referred to were actually made. [We find] no proof whatsoever that Dr. Cook reached the North Pole."[44]

With Cook declared a fraud and disgraced, Peary was able to bask in the glory of being first to the Arctic pole. However, over time it became clear that Peary's own claim was also shaky. First, he never produced any conclusive scientific evidence, such as observations of the sky made with his instruments, that he had made it closer than 150 miles (241km) from the pole. Also, several of the physical feats he had ascribed to himself and his men were later shown to be close to impossible. "Thirty miles per day was an unbelievable rate, even if the ice had been flat as a pancake," one expert points out, and the ice was actually riddled with obstacles such as ridges and cracks. Also:

Under no circumstances could he have completed the return journey in the time he claimed. [The] distance of almost 60 miles per day which he claimed for the southern journey are fantastical. Unless

This photo was taken during Peary's 1906 expedition, in which he failed to reach the North Pole but claimed to have made it to 87 degrees north.

Peary's Navigational Errors

In addition to reaching the North Pole himself in 1969, Walter "Wally" Herbert contributed to the debate about whether Robert Peary had actually been the first explorer to reach the pole. In his 1989 book The Noose of Laurels, *Herbert presents strong evidence that Peary never made it, including:*

An error in Peary's chronometer would also have affected his heading, and on his return to civilization it was found that his chronometer had indeed been ten minutes fast during the period he was making his journey. When his chronometer told him that the sun was on the Columbia meridian, the sun was therefore short of the transit by ten minutes. [Such an error] in aiming over a distance of 413 nautical miles would have put him west of the Pole by eighteen nautical miles. . . . By not taking observations for magnetic variation, the steering error would have increased the further north the party traveled, and as with all the other errors, they would have been drawing the party further and further to the west.

Wally Herbert, *The Noose of Laurels: Robert E. Peary and the Race to the North Pole.* New York: Atheneum, 1989, pp. 267–68.

Robert Peary offered his notes on the polar position of the sun as proof that he reached the North Pole. This proof is disputed because his chronometer was off by ten minutes and resulted in an error of 18 nautical miles.

Peary was a superman—and [his men] were supermen, too—he could not, by his own evidence, have done it.[45]

Making matters worse, U.S. congressional investigators looked into the matter in 1916. They said: "[Peary's] claims to the discoveries in the Arctic regions have been proven to rest on fiction and not on geographical facts."[46] It appeared that Peary's party had indeed made it into the heart of the Arctic. But he had missed the pole by many miles. Either he had made a genuine mistake in his calculations and thought he had made it to his goal; or, unable to find it, he had knowingly made a false claim. Whichever of these scenarios had actually occurred, Peary, like Cook, had been discredited.

First by Default

Eventually it became clear that if neither Cook nor Peary actually made it to the North Pole, by default the first reliably documented expedition to do so had to be credited as the first. That expedition was led by British explorer and writer Walter "Wally" Herbert. In 1968 he commanded a team that crossed some 3,800 miles (6,110km) of rugged, drifting ice and reached the pole on April 6, 1969, coincidentally on the sixtieth anniversary of Peary's famous 1909 trek. In an age of radar, television signals, satellites, and other advanced technology, no one doubted that Herbert's team had accomplished its goal. Worldwide acclaim was practically instantaneous, and he received numerous awards and medals, including the coveted Founder's Medal of the Royal Geographical Society.

Today, therefore, the general consensus of scientists and other experts is that Cook and Peary did not make it to the North Pole and that Herbert's expedition was the first to achieve that goal. A few defenders of Peary's priority still remain, however. As long as they hold on to the view that he was first, as scholar Clive Holland says, "the likelihood is that the debate about Peary's last journey [to the North Pole] will never end."[47]

Chapter Five

Antarctica in the Heroic Age

Although a great deal of attention was directed toward Arctic exploration in the late 1800s and early 1900s, interest in the Antarctic was no less fervid. In fact, in the same period in which two expeditions—Frederick Cook's and Robert Peary's—tried but failed to reach the North Pole, two others did make it to the South Pole. Historians and scientists date this extremely active era of south-polar activity from the last years of the nineteenth century to the early 1920s—about twenty-five years in total. It was marked by relentless attempts to cross the vast Antarctic continent by the explorers' own muscle power, aided by their sled dogs. Brave individuals faced extreme danger and privation, and several died. They were motivated partly by the desire to further their own reputations but also by the cause of science and expanding human knowledge. For these reasons, the era came to be called the Heroic Age of Antarctic exploration.

Another factor that made the age heroic was the frail, primitive nature (by today's standards) of the wooden ships the explorers used to reach the outer edges of the polar ice caps. Indeed, "it seems remarkable that those nineteenth-century sailors survived [the polar trips] at all," scholar John Maxtone-Graham remarks.

Their wooden sailing vessels offered primitive conditions: heat, light, and ventilation were inadequate, and a monotonous diet revolved exclusively around biscuit and salted meat. Sickness, injury, or death were inevitable [and ongoing risks in] a sailor's life. Though ships were strengthened for [polar] service, there was little protection for the crews who manned them [who consistently faced] frozen rigging, spume [spray] that literally sheathed seaman in icy [coatings, and] the continual risk of frostbite.[48]

Often making up in large degree for such dangers was the fortitude, skill, and courage of the officers and crews of the polar vessels. They were ready to press on as long as they had the slightest chance of accomplishing their goals. Swedish polar explorer Otto Nordenskiold captured their spirit when he said: "The demand of science, that no part of the globe shall remain untouched by the hand of investigation, was the force that drew our little band to the land of the farthest south."[49] Despite such determination, however, the explorers' ships could go only so far. Eventually, facing vast plains of pack ice or snow, the men had to strike out on foot, aided by their sledges and dogs.

"Little Human Insects"

When the Heroic Age began, it did so in earnest. Fifteen major expeditions headed for the Antarctic in the passage of fewer than twenty years. Explorers from several nations aimed either to explore various parts of the enormous southern continent or to conquer the South Pole, among them Norway,

The wooden sailing vessels early Antarctic explorers used offered primitive conditions: no heat, no light, bad ventilation, and lousy food as well as a propensity to get stuck and crushed in the ice.

Belgium, Germany, Scotland, France, Japan, Australia, and Britain. All felt that major exploration of the Antarctic was overdue. Meteorologists, oceanographers, geologists, biologists, and numerous other scientists complained that they knew practically nothing about the southern continent. It was time, they said, to explore its frozen reaches in as much detail as possible.

Belgian explorer Adrien de Gerlache led an expedition to Antarctica in 1898 and was the first to spend an entire winter inside the Antarctic Circle.

Of the long list of nations that strove to explore Antarctica, Britain swiftly took the lead. This was partly because the British had been building a worldwide empire throughout the nineteenth century. They had numerous thriving colonies in southern regions, including Cape Town, in southern Africa, and Australia and New Zealand, in the southern Pacific. In British eyes it seemed only natural that the southernmost continent should become still another extension of British power and influence.

The British quickly learned that they had their work cut out for them, however, as their rivals tried hard to outdo them. One of the most ambitious non-British expeditions was mounted and led by Belgian naval officer Adrien de Gerlache. His first mate was Norway's champion explorer Roald Amundsen, and the party's surgeon was Frederick Cook, who would later make a much bigger name for himself in Arctic exploration. Financed by the Belgian government, the expedition departed from Antwerp in 1897 and reached Antarctica early in 1898.

Soon the ship, the *Belgica*, became trapped in pack ice off the coast. As a result, the expedition became the first to spend an entire winter inside the Antarctic Circle. This exposed the crew to extremely rigorous conditions for many months. In addition to the freezing cold and monotonous diet, the men endured long stretches of darkness, and the lack of sunlight caused serious bouts of depression. Fortunately, Cook came up with the idea of having them

Antarctic Explorers' Routes

70° S

Ross Sea

Victoria Land

Ross Island

Bay of Whales

Robert Falcon Scott, Edward Wilson, and H.R. Bowers die (about 03/30/1912)

Ross Ice Shelf

Edgar Evans dies (03/17/1912)

Lawrence Oates dies (03/17/1912)

Beardmore Glacier

Axel Heiberg Glacier

Ernest Shackleton turns back (01/09/1909)

50° S

Scott (01/17/1912)

Roald Amundsen (12/14/1911)

South Pole

═══ Shackleton's Route   ═══ Amundsen's Route   ═══ Scott's Route

stare for extended periods into bright wood fires, which helped to alleviate their melancholy. At winter's end, the exhausted men managed to break out of the ice and return to Belgium.

Not to be outdone by the Belgians, the British launched their first large-scale Antarctic voyage of the era in 1901. The "Discovery" expedition, like other polar journeys named for their ships, was led by one of the greatest of all polar explorers—Robert Falcon Scott. Born into a seagoing family in southwestern England in 1868, he joined the British navy in his teens. Life aboard ship suited him, and he quick-ly became a highly disciplined hard worker as well as a natural leader. The

Captain Robert Falcon Scott, at head of table, celebrates his birthday with members of his Terra Nova expedition in Antarctica in 1911.

physicist on the Discovery expedition, Louis Bernacchi, later wrote:

> Captain Scott, with his striking personality and charm of manner, his courage, his enthusiasm for science, had the ability to inspire loyalty and devotion. He had understanding and knowledge and never failed to stand up for what he considered right. [He was] an ideal leader for such an expedition—although he had his weaknesses, too, for he was very human.[50]

About those weaknesses, one historian said that Scott's charm masked "a psychological turmoil . . . [for] beneath that reasoned exterior lurked those familiar demons—[a] violent temper, black depression, [and] insecurity with his peers."[51]

Scott's Discovery expedition, which was sponsored by the Royal Society and Royal Geographical Society, did not set out to reach the South Pole. Rather, the goal was to collect as much geographical and other scientific data as possible about Antarctica. Among the party were several young explorers who would later lead their own polar expeditions, most prominently the English-Irish adventurer Ernest Shackleton. The men reached latitude 82° south, setting a new record, and mapped many previously unknown geographical features. They were also first to see the vast plateau that makes up much of the Antarctic continent. Seeing it as so huge and desolate that it made humans seem insignificant, Scott was moved to say: "[Before us stretches] nothing but this terrible limitless expanse of snow, [and] we, little human insects, have started to crawl over this awful desert."[52]

Shackleton and the *Nimrod*

During the Discovery trek, Shackleton came down with scurvy, a debilitating condition caused by lack of vitamin C. To his great regret, he had to be sent home early and afterward longed to return to the Antarctic, hopefully at the head of his own expedition. His dream came true when three years later he managed to get private funding ($100,000, a very large sum at the time) for what became known as the Nimrod expedition. Departing in July 1907, the *Nimrod* made good time to the southern continent and anchored in McMurdo Sound, bordering Victoria Land and the Ross Ice Shelf.

Shackleton had planned an ambitious, multipurpose exploratory program. He hoped to explore both new and known large-scale geographical features, as well as to reach both the geographical South Pole and magnetic South Pole. Several of these goals were successfully attained. In March 1908 members of the party climbed to the summit of the huge volcano Mt. Erebus, on Ross Island (off the coast of Victoria Land). Soon afterward, another crewman, Australian Douglas Mawson, and two companions hiked across Victoria Land and located the magnetic South Pole (which slowly changes position over time).

Meanwhile, Shackleton himself, along with three other men, headed toward the continent's interior, intent on reaching the geographical South Pole. Well behind and above the Ross Ice Shelf, they found and named Beardmore Glacier, an enormous moving ice floe jammed between two mountain ranges. Modern Antarctic researcher Michael Rosove describes the "almost incomprehensible difficulty" the men experienced in scaling the glacier:

> The men encountered chaotic surfaces and fell repeatedly, but fortunately sustained only minor injuries. Crevasses [deep cracks] of enormous dimension and unfathomable depth were encountered, concealed by deceptive [coatings of snow]. The men were hauling a total weight of about one thousand pounds [and] the work became increasingly exhausting with the [increasing] altitude.[53]

After making it to the top of the glacier, Shackleton and his companions saw the immense Antarctic plain spreading out before them. They set out for the pole, some 500 miles (805km) distant, with confidence. But ultimately they

Shackleton, the Consummate Leader

Scholar Michael Rosove provides this excellent summary of the background and strengths of the great polar explorer Ernest Shackleton:

Shackleton was from Yorkshire [in northeastern England], of Anglo-Irish origin. He found school boring but enjoyed the solitude of reading. He was hardy and favored adventure, and was well-matched to the rigorous requirements of sailing ships. . . . At age twenty-four he was certified as sailing master and three years later he was selected to be third mate on [Scott's] *Discovery* expedition. [He] proved himself capable and probably too popular for Scott, who sent him home on account of ill health. Shackleton was part poet/philosopher, part romantic, and part renegade. [His] charisma [charm], optimism, and determination were unassailable [unarguable]. At sea and in the wild places of the world he was the consummate [perfect] leader, inspiring confidence and loyalty in men who served him again and again.

Michael H. Rosove, ed., *Let Heroes Speak: Antarctic Explorers, 1772–1922.* Annapolis, MD: Naval Institute Press, 2000, pp. 146–47.

Ernest Shackleton, second from left, poses with some of his expedition members on board the Nimrod *in the Antarctic Circle. The harsh conditions they endured in the Antarctic are etched in their faces.*

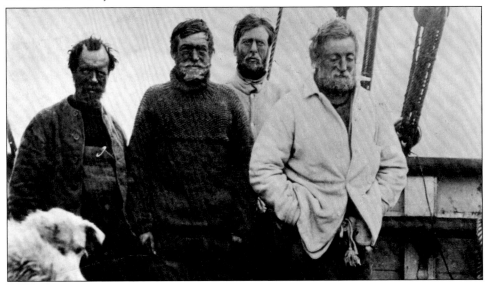

Roald Amundsen's ship, the Fram, *was an engine-equipped sailing ship suited for ice pack and Antarctic travel.*

lacked the supplies and stamina to make it all the way. Turning back on January 9, 1909, Shackleton wrote: "Whatever regrets may be, we have done our best."[54] This, it turned out, was an understatement. The four men had made it to latitude 88° south, a mere 97 miles (156km) from the South Pole, the closest anyone had ever gotten to it up to that time.

"The Goal Was Achieved"

It was not long before two other explorers surpassed Shackleton's milestone on the road to the South Pole. By the time Shackleton had returned to Britain in 1904, Scott was already planning his own journey to the pole. Meanwhile, Amundsen had also set his sights on the North Pole. However, in 1909 news came that Peary had made it to the top of the world. So Amundsen immediately changed his plans and targeted the South Pole instead. He kept it a secret for some time, not even telling his crew until the expedition was well under way. He was not disappointed at having to change his destination. From childhood, he had dreamed of becoming an explorer and of conquering the geographical poles. So, finding that one of them was no longer available, he had no trouble targeting the other instead.

Amundsen's ship, the *Fram*, headed southward in August 1910. Out of professional courtesy, he felt obliged to inform Scott but waited until October 12.

The telegram read simply: "Am going south, Amundsen."[55] Scott denied that he was bothered about suddenly finding himself in competition with one of the leading polar explorers in the world; but in truth, he may well have been worried that Amundsen might beat him to the prize.

The *Fram* reached the Bay of Whales, in front of the Ross Ice Shelf, on January 14, 1911. Then, traveling by sledge, Amundsen spent several months finding a suitable route to the pole and laying down caches of supplies at strategic points. The route he selected—over the Axel Heiberg Glacier (a few hundred miles from the Beardmore Glacier)—was previously unknown.

Finally, on October 19 he took three other men, four sledges, and fifty-two dogs and struck out for the pole. Eventually, the four men passed Shackleton's farthest point south, an event that excited them so much that they briefly stopped to celebrate and pay homage to the intrepid explorer whom they felt had blazed the way for them. Amundsen later recalled: "We did not pass that spot without according our highest tribute of admiration to the man, who—together with his gallant companions—had planted his country's

An Extremely Close Call

Amundsen's 1911 try for the South Pole was fraught with danger. In this excerpt from his own account of the journey, he describes an extremely close call when one of his men almost disappeared forever into a crevasse (deep crack in the ice):

Suddenly we saw Bjaaland's sledge sink over. He jumped off and seized the [rope], The sledge lay on its side for a few seconds, then began to sink more and more, and finally disappeared altogether. . . . All this happened in [only] a few moments. "Now I can't hold on any longer!" [he cried out]. He was holding on convulsively, and resisting with all his force, but it was no use. Inch by inch the sledge sank deeper. The dogs, too, seemed to understand the gravity of the situation. [They] dug their claws in and resisted with all their strength. But still . . . slowly but surely, it went down into the abyss. . . . A few seconds more and his sledge and thirteen dogs would never have seen the light of day again. Help came at the last moment. Hanssen and Hassel [had] snatched an Alpine rope [and] came to his assistance.

Roald Amundsen, *The South Pole: An Account of the Norwegian Antarctic Expedition in the* Fram, *1910–1912,* Part II. New York: Cooper Square, 2001, pp. 6–7.

flag nearer to the goal than any of his precursors."[56]

Amundsen and his companions reached the South Pole on December 14, 1911. He later wrote:

At three in the afternoon, a simultaneous "Halt!" rang out from the drivers. They had carefully examined their sledge-meters, and they all showed the full distance—our Pole by reckoning. The goal was achieved, the journey ended. . . . The object of my life was attained. [After] we had halted, we collected and congratulated each other. [Then] we proceeded to the greatest and most solemn act of the whole journey—the planting of our flag. . . . I had determined that the act of planting it—the historic event— should be equally divided among us all. It was not for one man to do this. It was for *all* who had staked their lives in the struggle.[57]

"We Shall Stick It Out to the End"

Scott's attempt to reach the pole was far more difficult and less congenial than Amundsen's. The so-called Terra Nova expedition, with Scott in command, sailed southward late in 1910 and reached McMurdo Sound in January 1911. Many months of preparations followed until Scott felt he was ready to strike out for the pole. At the last minute, he selected four companions—a doctor, Edward Wilson; two sailors, Edgar

Evans and H.R. Bowers; and an army officer, Lawrence Oates, nicknamed "Titus." Experts later deemed Scott's decision to take four instead of three men with him a mistake. The party's provisions had been planned for four men, and adding a fifth meant that each would have to do with a bit less.

As they left for the pole on November 1, 1911, Scott and his men were already about two weeks behind Amundsen, who had departed for the same objective on October 19. Unfortunately for the Terra Nova party, as the days wore on they fell increasingly farther behind. In large part this was because they were beset by one storm after another, which both slowed and exhausted them. In contrast, Amundsen had encountered mostly calm weather.

Finally, on January 17, 1912, Scott and his companions reached the pole. But what should have been a joyous occasion turned out to be bitterly disappointing, as Scott told it in his diary:

The worst has happened, or nearly the worst. We marched well into the morning [and] we started off in high spirits [but] about the second hour of the march, Bowers's sharp eyes detected . . . a black speck ahead. [We] marched on [and] found that it was a black flag tied to a sledge bearer; nearby [was] the remains of a camp, [with] sledge tracks and ski tracks going and coming and the clear trace of dogs' paws—many dogs. This told us the whole story. The Norwegians have forestalled us and are first to the Pole. It is a terrible disappointment, and I am very sorry for my loyal companions.[58]

Wasting little time, Scott ordered a retreat to the nearest of his supply bases. Unfortunately for him and his men, the return trip turned out to be horrendous. Not only were they in low spirits, they were frostbitten and weak, and their pace drastically slowed down to only a few miles a day. On February 17 Evans collapsed. Unable to walk any farther, he died that night, perhaps of exhaustion, or the cold, or both. Exactly a month later, on March 17, Oates, dazed and clearly not himself, got up in the middle of the night, left the tent, and walked away into a snowstorm. Scott wrote: "We knew that poor Oates was walking to his death, but though we tried to dissuade him, we knew it was the act of a brave man. We all hope to meet the end with a similar spirit."[59]

Making matters worse, inclement weather again set in. On March 19, when the party was only 11 miles (18km) from the supply base and safety, a huge blizzard struck. The three remaining men, confined to their tent, grew weaker and weaker. Realizing they were not going to make it, they wrote final messages to loved ones and waited for the blizzard's end, which for them never came. Scott's last message, probably written on March 29, the day of his passing, read: "I do not think we can hope for any better things now. We shall stick it out to the end, but we are getting weaker. . . . It seems a pity, but I do not think I can write more. R. Scott. For God's sake, look after our people."[60]

A Case of Bad Luck?

On November 12, 1912, a little more than seven months after the three explorers perished, a rescue party found the tent. Inside, Scott, Bowers, and Wilson were perfectly preserved by the perpetual Antarctic cold and lying in the exact positions they had been in when they had breathed their last. Feeling it inappropriate to move the fallen heroes, the rescuers took out the poles that held up the tent and allowed it to drape down over the bodies. Then they built a memorial mound of snow above it and placed a cross composed of two skis at the top. "There alone in their greatness they will lie," one of the rescuers said, "with the most fitting tomb in the world above them."[61]

For a long time after the tragedy, explorers and other experts debated the reasons it had occurred. Theories abounded. Besides the fact that Scott's food rations were inadequate, some suggested that he had made a major error in taking no dogs on the last leg of the journey. Amundsen had taken many dogs, some of which he and his men had eaten along the way. In comparison, having no dogs, Scott and his men had to haul all the supplies themselves and lacked the extra food source that some of the animals would have provided.

Even more telling, however, is a more recent theory that proposes that a freak

A replica of the tent in which a rescue party found the frozen bodies of explorers Scott, Bowers, and Wilson.

weather pattern doomed Scott. Susan Solomon, a scientist with the National Oceanic and Atmospheric Administration, has thoroughly researched Scott's last expedition. She points to some recent studies of past Antarctic temperatures, especially those in early 1912, when Scott and his men were on their way back from the pole. The data, she says, shows that 1912 was an abnormally cold and stormy year, even for Antarctica:

[The studies] demonstrate that Scott and his party were fighting for their lives under rare conditions that were surely very much colder than normal. [They] struggled through three weeks when almost every daily minimum temperature was a bitter and debilitating 10 to 20 degrees F colder than what can now be shown to be typical, based on many years of observations in this region. . . . The temperatures had taken a sharp and unusual turn for the worse, and with them went Scott's chances for survival. [It is likely that] Scott and his men endured a highly unusual twist of fate.[62]

"She's Gone, Boys"

During Ernest Shackleton's 1914 Antarctic expedition, his ship, the *Endurance*, was crushed in the ice. One of his men later recalled its disappearance beneath the freezing surface:

> There was our poor ship . . . struggling in her death-agony. She went down bow first, her stern raised in the air. She then gave one quick dive and the ice closed over her forever. It gave one a sickening sensation to see it, for, mastless and useless as she was, she seemed to be a link with the outer world. . . . I doubt if there was one amongst us who did not feel some personal emotion when Sir Ernest, standing on the top of the look-out, said somewhat sadly and quietly, "She's gone, boys."

Afterward, Shackleton and his men made an incredibly hazardous journey across hundreds of miles of ice and rough seas before finally reaching safety.

Quoted in Ernest Shackleton, *South: The Last Antarctic Expedition of Shackleton and the* Endurance. New York: Lyons, 1998, pp. 98–99.

Like many ships before her, Shackleton's Endurance *lies trapped in the ice before being slowly crushed, as depicted in this 1915 photo.*

More than anything else, therefore, the tragedy that struck the Terra Nova expedition may have been, simply put, a case of bad luck. If so, the incident underscored the extreme dangers involved in polar exploration and the tremendous risks the explorers in prior eras took. Moreover, they were completely willing to take such risks without regret or shame. Scott himself summed up this heroic ethic concisely and quite beautifully in his last message to the public, written in the tent that would become his tomb. "I do not regret this journey," he said. "We took risks. We knew we took them. Things have come out against us, and therefore we have no cause for complaint."[63]

Chapter Six

The Age of Mechanized Exploration

Shortly after Roald Amundsen's and Robert Falcon Scott's epic race for the South Pole ended in triumph for one and tragedy for the other, World War I began. During that mammoth struggle, lasting from 1914 to 1918, polar exploration virtually halted, as most resources needed for expeditions went into the war effort. When the conflict ended, exploration resumed. But its nature had fundamentally and permanently changed. Old-style wooden sailing ships were fast being replaced by more modern metal vessels, and a wide range of mechanized transports promised new, faster ways to cross the barren polar ice fields. As Holland explains:

> The war period, and the years immediately following it, brought major technological advances which completely changed the face of [polar] exploration, and stimulated a whole new era of attempts

to attain the [poles]. The object now was not to be the first to get there, but to be the first to get there by other means. From the 1920s onwards, polar explorers had at their disposal a new generation of aircraft, airships [also called dirigibles, zeppelins, or blimps], icebreakers, submarines, and motorized land transport [including tractors and snowmobiles], all of which were rapidly becoming more reliable, more powerful, and safe enough to be deemed suitable for use in remote areas.[64]

Flight of the *Eagle*

Actually, the idea of reaching the poles by means other than walking was not completely new to the post–World War I explorers. Even before the turn of the twentieth century, for example, a few forward-thinking individuals realized that flying to the poles through the air would be potentially faster and safer than traveling through the difficult terrain. At the time, no airplanes yet existed. But people had been flying aloft in balloons for decades.

So in 1897 a Swedish engineer named Salomon A. Andre tried to reach the North Pole in a silk balloon filled with hydrogen gas. He named it the *Eagle*. Taking along two companions, Andre left Spitzbergen Island on July 11 and immediately encountered trouble. He had designed the craft so that long ropes would hang down and drag along the ground, giving the balloonists a crude means of steering. But the ropes broke away right at the beginning of the flight. As one eyewitness later commented:

> The loss of the guidelines caused the whole of the balloon journey to take place altogether in another way than had been intended, for the travelers now found themselves in an almost ordinary free balloon which would be compelled to obey the direction of the wind.[65]

After drifting a bit more than 300 miles (483km), the *Eagle* crash-landed on an ice floe in the middle of the Arctic Ocean. The men managed to survive for a few months but eventually succumbed to starvation and exposure. Their skeletons, along with Andre's diary, describing the ordeal, were discovered by Norwegian seal hunters thirty-three years later.

In 1897 Sweden's Salomon A. Andre launched the Eagle, *his hydrogen-filled silk balloon, in an attempt to reach the North Pole. He landed three hundred miles away on an ice floe. Seal hunters found his body thirty-three years later.*

"Shall We Be Thought Mad?"

During his 1897 attempt to reach the North Pole in a balloon, Salomon Andre described how he felt floating through the Arctic wilderness:

Is it not a little strange to be floating here above the polar sea? To be the first that have floated here in a balloon? How soon, I wonder, shall we have successors? Shall we be thought mad or will our example be followed? I cannot deny that all three of us are dominated by a feeling of pride. We think we can well face death, having done what we have done. Isn't it all, perhaps, the expression of an extremely strong sense of individuality which cannot bear the thought of living and dying like a man in the ranks, forgotten by coming generations? Is this ambition?

Quoted in Pierre Berton, *Arctic Grail: The Quest for the Northwest Passage and the North Pole, 1818–1909.* New York: Lyons, 2000, p. 508.

Airplanes Prove Their Potential

Andre's fatal mishap had shown that balloons were not strong and reliable enough to withstand the daunting polar distances and elements. But airplanes, which became increasingly sophisticated after World War I, proved a good deal more dependable. Indeed, they appeared particularly promising for delivering explorers and supplies to distant, dangerous locations. Aviator and scholar C.V. Glines tells why polar explorers preferred to use the airplane as a form of transport instead of undertaking long journeys by foot and sledge:

The enormous difficulties experienced by ground-bound explorers, not only in finding a way over the snow and ice, but in the constant struggle against cold and starvation, could be avoided. Distances, which on foot would take weeks or even months, could be covered in mere hours. True, there were risks and dangers in the air, but they could hardly be greater than those on the ground.[66]

The potential of airplanes for polar journeys was not lost on Amundsen, who had already cemented his reputation by being the first to walk to the South Pole. In 1922 he planned to fly a small, single-engine aircraft from Alaska over the North Pole to Spitzbergen. But the plane was badly damaged during test flights, and the expedition had to be abandoned. Amundsen tried again in 1925, this time taking two planes, along with wealthy American businessman Lincoln Ellsworth. They made it to within 136 miles (213km) of the pole before engine failure in one of the planes forced them to turn back. Although the attempt failed, it was seen as important because it proved that airplanes could successfully operate in the freezing polar environment.

Polar aviation seemed to start to come of age the following year. Admiral Richard E. Byrd claimed that he, along with his pilot Floyd Bennett, had managed to fly over the North Pole. Byrd later wrote: "At 9:02 am, May 9, 1926 . . . our calculations showed us to be at the Pole! The dream of a lifetime had at last been realized."[67]

Byrd was long hailed, both in public and in the history books, for this feat. However, some doubts later surfaced about whether he had actually reached the North Pole that year. Some aviation experts suggested that Byrd's and Bennett's estimates of the plane's velocity and/or their direction were incorrect.

Richard E. Byrd and pilot Floyd Bennett flew the Miss Josephine Byrd *over the North Pole on May 9, 1926. The accomplishment is disputed by some historians.*

If so, they may have flown in large circles in an area at least several dozen miles from the pole. Moreover, in 1996 Byrd's diary from the 1926 flight was finally released. On close examination, it showed some strange erasures that some experts suspected were attempts to cover up the fact that he had not reached the objective due to an oil leak or some other malfunction. A few supporters of Byrd's claim still linger, however. So the matter has never been settled completely.

If indeed Byrd was not the first to fly over the pole, that honor would have to go to Amundsen and Italian inventor Umberto Nobile. On May 11, 1926, just two days after the Byrd-Bennett flight, they flew Nobile's airship, the *Norge*, over the North Pole. In the decade or so that followed, however, dirigibles proved to be not only considerably slower than airplanes but also prone to accidents, including gas explosions. After Nobile's second polar airship, the *Italia*, went down with the loss of several crewmen in 1928, airships were largely abandoned by polar explorers.

Byrd at the South Pole

Despite the failure of the *Italia*, 1928 turned out to be a banner year for the use of aircraft and other mechanized vehicles in polar exploration. Still basking in the glory of his supposed flyover of the North Pole two years before, Byrd launched an all-out mechanized expedition to the South Pole. He managed to raise $800,000 to finance a mission featuring the latest advances in modern

Roald Amundsen and inventor Umberto Nobile flew Nobile's airship, the Norge, *over the North Pole on May 11, 1926, two days after Byrd's and Bennett's flight.*

machines; they included four airplanes, a large tractor, two steam-powered ships (one with a metal hull), several snowmobiles, and some radio transmitters. Arriving at the Ross Ice Shelf, Byrd ordered his crew, containing more than sixty men, to construct a small village to act as a base camp. He called it Little America.

The highlight of the expedition was an attempt to fly over the geographical South Pole. Byrd had earlier said, "Aviation cannot claim mastery of the globe until the South Pole and its vast surrounding mystery be opened up by airplane."[68] He now tried to make good on these words. The plane chosen, dubbed the *Floyd Bennett* after Byrd's former pilot and friend who had recently died, possessed a then impressive 1,000 horsepower and a top speed of 122 miles (196km) per hour. Veteran pilot Bernt Balchen was at the controls, while Byrd navigated. Early in the morning of November 19, 1929, after a ten-hour flight, the plane reached its goal, an achievement that has never been challenged. "The Pole, the mysterious objective, was actually in sight," Byrd later wrote.

> At 1:14 o'clock, Greenwich Civil Time, our calculations showed that we were at the Pole. We turned right and flew three or four miles. Had we turned right just before reaching the Pole, one could say that we had turned westward. But having reached the Pole, we really turned northward, because all directions at the South Pole are north. . . . For a few seconds we [hovered] over the

spot where Amundsen had stood [and] where Scott had also stood. . . . In their honor, the flags of their countries were again carried over the Pole. [Then] we put the Pole behind us and raced for home.[69]

Byrd followed up his triumph with a second highly mechanized expedition to Antarctica. In January 1934 he reached the site of the first Little America, which by now was partly buried in snow drifts. He told his men to dig out some of the buildings and to erect others. This time he did not try for the pole, instead concentrating on geographical exploration and meteorological research. Snowmobiles, airplanes, and a new addition—a helicopter—fanned out across nearby sectors of the southern continent, greatly expanding knowledge about it.

Still More Technological Advances

In the years that followed, the pace of mechanization of polar exploration and research accelerated. In 1937, for instance, four Russian planes landed at the North Pole, the first time anyone had accomplished that feat. (The first landing of an aircraft at the South Pole took place much later, in 1956.) Also, in 1940 Byrd launched still another Antarctic expedition, this time sponsored by the U.S. government. Once more, all manner of motorized transports and the latest electronic survey and communications equipment were utilized.

At the same time, a number of countries began to express an interest in

Byrd Inaugurates Little America

When Richard Byrd reached the Ross Ice Shelf in Antarctica, his men began erecting a village-like camp. One of these men, Norman D. Vaughan, later remembered how Byrd inaugurated and named it:

As our first task, Byrd ordered us to do something that remains one of my special memories. I unpacked two shovels from the sled. Byrd took one and handed Balchen the other. They started to dig. Then Strom and I took turns. We all wanted to be part of the momentous occasion. From the ice we cut out chunks roughly a cubic foot in size. We piled them one on top of another until they stood six feet high. Byrd then unfurled the American flag. Using a ski pole as a mast, he hoisted the colors. "Shipmates," said the commander, with his eyes glowing, "today, December 27, 1928, I name this Little America. May this flag wave here forever!"

Norman D. Vaughan, *With Byrd at the Bottom of the World: The South Pole Expedition of 1928–1930*. Harrisburg, PA: Stackpole, 1990, pp. 41–42.

Only poles and masts of a ship buried in the snow could be seen at Admiral Byrd's Little America Camp in 1934.

laying claim to various sections of the southern continent. The U.S. government worried that with World War II ongoing, Germany and other hostile nations might try to use Antarctica for strategic military purposes. The Americans strongly felt that that continent should be an international territory owned by no one. But President Franklin D. Roosevelt opted to keep an American presence in the region, at least in part to safeguard it from enemy exploitation. He placed Byrd in charge of upcoming Antarctic operations.

These plans were temporarily put on hold when the United States entered the conflict in 1941. But at the close of the war the Americans returned in force. In 1946, backed by the U.S. Navy, Byrd arrived in Antarctica with a massive armada of forty-seven hundred men, thirteen modern ships, and numerous airplanes, helicopters, tractors, snowmobiles, and other motorized equipment. Dubbed Operation Highjump, the expedition was intended to maintain U.S. presence in the area, to investigate previously unexplored regions, and to determine the feasibility of establishing permanent Antarctic bases.

The next two decades witnessed still more technological advances that were subsequently applied to polar exploration. In particular, icebreakers (vessels designed to break up ice as they move along) and nuclear submarines revolutionized transportation to and from the poles. In 1958 the USS *Nautilus*, the world's first nuclear sub, passed beneath the north-polar ice cap. After reaching

the geographical North Pole, the ship traveled to Greenland, where it resurfaced.

The *Nautilus*'s voyage was staged as part of the International Geophysical Year (IGY). Lasting from July 1, 1957, to December 31, 1958, it was an enormous effort by more than seventy nations to gather scientific information. Huge amounts of data were collected about geology, geomagnetism, gravity, atmospheric physics, meteorology, oceanography, seismology, cosmic rays, and solar activity, and much of this information came from polar researchers.

The largest polar expedition of the IGY was the Commonwealth Trans-Antarctic Expedition, sponsored by the United Kingdom, New Zealand, the United States, Australia, and South Africa. It was led by New Zealand's Edmund Hillary (who had earlier been the first person to climb the highest peak in the world, Mt. Everest), and Britain's Vivian Fuchs (who, despite the first name, was a man). The expedition made history by accomplishing the first crossing of the entire continent via the geographical South Pole. Two groups, led by Hillary and Fuchs respectively, approached the pole from opposite directions. When Hillary reached it on January 3, 1958, his was only the third team—after Amundsen's and Scott's—to reach it by ground-based travel, often called a surface traverse. (The major difference was that Amundsen and Scott had done it by foot and sledge only, whereas Hillary had tractors and other sophisticated machines. The 1958 teams also had the benefit of many supply depots laid along their routes by both airplanes and tractors.)

"That Unquenchable Power"

Although by 1958 four teams of explorers (counting Fuchs's party) had reached the South Pole by surface traverse, no one had yet made it to the North Pole that way. It was not until a decade later that that record was finally shattered. In 1968 an American team of four led by Minnesota native Ralph Plaisted set out to reach the top of the world by snowmobile. Leaving Ward Hunt Island (near Ellesmere Island) on March 9, they covered 412 miles (663 km) in forty-three days and arrived at the pole on April 19. Their feat was confirmed by a U.S. Air Force aircraft that flew overhead.

Of course, Plaisted and his companions did have the advantage of riding in mechanized vehicles, something that the polar explorers of the nineteenth century and before could only dream about. The

In 1968 Minnesota insurance salesman Ralph Plaisted led a four-man expedition on snowmobiles to the North Pole.

1968 expedition also benefited from airplane drops of gasoline and other supplies along the way. Wally Herbert's historic polar trip, which took place the following year, sought to eliminate these advantages and try to reach the pole the same way that the men of Frederick Cook's, Robert Peary's, Roald Amundsen's and Robert Falcon Scott's era had. For that reason, Herbert's expedition is credited with being the first to reach that goal unaided by modern motorized equipment.

Herbert's expedition was by no means the last to claim a "first" in polar journeys. All manner of means, some including mechanized equipment and some not, were used in the years that followed. To name only a few: In 1975 the Soviet Union's *Arktika* became the first icebreaker to reach the North Pole; in 1982 Ranulph Fiennes and Charles Burton were first to cross the Arctic Ocean in a single season; in 1988 a joint Soviet-Canadian team was first to reach the North Pole on skis, aided by satellite communications; in 2005 six men comprising the so-called Ice Challenger Expedition were first to make it to the South Pole in a six-wheel-drive vehicle; in 2007 a team sponsored by the British Broadcasting Company (BBC) was first to travel to the magnetic North Pole by car; and in 2009 in the Kapersky Commonwealth Antarctic Expedition, seven women from various nations skied to the geographical South Pole in thirty-eight days.

These and other diverse polar ventures demonstrate clearly that the appeal of conquering the frozen lands at the top and bottom of the world has not dimmed. No matter how many people have gone before, others want to follow, often using the newest methods available. Mawson describes what he saw as the motivation that drives them all: "The desire for the pure elements of natural revelation [discovery] lay at the source of that unquenchable power—the love of adventure!"[70]

To Conquer the Unknown: Modern Polar Research

The worries expressed by American leaders in the 1930s and 1940s about the seizure and exploitation of Antarctic territories by various nations became more pronounced after World War II. Some countries claimed pieces of the southern continent, almost as the explorers of prior eras, such as Christopher Columbus, had claimed newly found lands for their own nations. By contrast, other countries, especially the United States, continually pushed for an international agreement that would ban such claims. The goal was to ensure that Antarctica would be set aside as an international preserve and used only for peaceful purposes, particularly for scientific research.

This goal was achieved in 1959 with the creation of the Antarctic Treaty. It was signed by representatives from the twelve nations that had accomplished most of the exploration and research in the region up to that time. They were Argentina, Australia, Belgium, Chile, France, Japan, New Zealand, Norway, South Africa, the Soviet Union, the United Kingdom (Britain), and the United States. (Since that time, thirty-four other nations have signed it, making a total of forty-six, which together support more than 80 percent of Earth's population.) The agreement forbade any and all military operations on the continent, including nuclear tests and the storage of radioactive wastes. It also made Antarctica an international territory free from individual national ownership and encouraged the construction of research stations for the purpose of scientific investigation.

No such treaty has yet been created for the northern polar region. Until 1999 the international community had verbally agreed that no single nation owned the North Pole. After that date a few countries tried to lay claim to either the pole or the seabed beneath it. But the issue remains disputed and unresolved. In the meantime, in the spirit of the pioneers of the past, exploration, in the form of scientific research, remains ongoing in both polar regions, particularly in Antarctica.

Antarctic and Arctic Stations

Antarctic bases had been constructed both during and after the continent's Heroic Age of exploration. Byrd's Little America, which was rebuilt several times, was a prominent example. But these stations were invariably abandoned when the expeditions that built them were over. After Operation Highjump studied the potential of permanent bases in the mid-1940s, the United States set its sights on building some. In 1956, in anticipation of the upcoming International Geophysical Year (IGY), the U.S. Navy erected the first permanent base at the South Pole. Appropriately, it was named the Amundsen-Scott South Pole Station after the first men to stand on that exceedingly remote spot. Both Edmund Hillary and Vivian Fuchs reached and rested at the then fairly new station during their polar journeys in 1958.

The base, which was rebuilt twice after that, has been continually occupied ever since. It lies 330 feet (100m) from the geographical South Pole and at an elevation of 9,301 feet (2,835m) above sea level. About two hundred scientists and other personnel work there in the summer and from forty to fifty in the winter. They conduct experiments in geophysics, astronomy, meteorology, atmospheric physics, and some biomedical areas.

The Amundsen-Scott station is not the only permanent base in Antarctica. In all, thirty countries presently operate more than sixty stations there. Together, they house about four thousand people in the summer and about a thousand in the winter. The largest of all is the U.S.-run McMurdo Station, on the coast of Ross Island, established soon after the Amundsen-Scott base in 1956. McMurdo boasts more than a hundred structures, a harbor, an airfield, a helicopter pad, a large science center, an aquarium, extensive telephone lines, and a sewer system. Some twelve hundred people inhabit the station during the summer; roughly two hundred do so in the winter.

In addition, over the years a few research stations were built in the Arctic region. These were called "drifting stations" because the ice pack on which they were constructed steadily moves through the Arctic Ocean. Thus, though some lasted for a few years, they eventually succumbed to the elements and therefore were not permanent.

The first Arctic drifting station was erected by the Soviets in 1937. The Americans' first versions, called Alpha and Bravo, were built in the late 1950s as part of the IGY initiative. Each housed from twenty to thirty scientists and military personnel at any given time. After these two outposts had to be abandoned, others were erected in the 1960s. Meanwhile, the Soviets kept two or more Arctic stations operating almost yearly until 1991, when the Soviet Union collapsed. Then, after a lapse of more than a decade, Russia deployed a few of these

"To Promote International Cooperation"

The 1959 Antarctic Treaty made Antarctica an international zone. The first three articles of the document are as follows:

Article I, Peaceful Purposes

1. Antarctica shall be used for peaceful purposes only. There shall be prohibited . . . any measure of a military nature, such as the establishment of military bases and fortifications, the carrying out of military maneuvers, as well as the testing of any type of weapon.
2. The present Treaty shall not prevent the use of military personnel or equipment for scientific research or for any other peaceful purpose.

Article II, Freedom of Scientific Investigation

Freedom of scientific investigation in Antarctica and cooperation toward that end, as applied during the International Geophysical Year, shall continue, subject to the provisions of the present Treaty.

Article III, International Scientific Cooperation

1. In order to promote international cooperation in scientific investigation in Antarctica, as provided for in Article II of the present Treaty, the Contracting Parties agree that, to the greatest extent feasible and practicable:
   a. information regarding plans for scientific programs in Antarctica shall be exchanged to permit maximum economy of and efficiency of operations;
   b. scientific personnel shall be exchanged in Antarctica between expeditions and stations;
   c. scientific observations and results from Antarctica shall be exchanged and made freely available.

British Antarctic Survey, "The Antarctic Treaty." www.antarctica.ac.uk/about_antarctica/geopolitical/treaty/update_1959.php.

stations between 2003 and 2008. But they were eventually abandoned due to rapid melting of the Arctic ice pack caused by global climate change.

However, this does not mean that research in the area is over for good.

Some scientists, including a number in the United States, have proposed building floating platforms, similar to modern oil rigs, to do scientific research in the Arctic region. Preliminary designs have already been drawn up.

From Darkness Toward Light

In Antarctica, in the meantime, the march of science and human knowledge continues without interruption. Experts heavily involved in this research have their disagreements, but all agree that polar exploration, which began centuries ago in frail wooden ships piloted by risk takers searching for what lay beyond the horizon, will go on for many generations to come. Like those daring pioneers, modern polar explorers and researchers believe that the desire to conquer the unknown is an inherent part of the human makeup. They concur with Nobel Prize–winning Norwegian explorer Fridtjof Nansen (1861–1930), who said:

> People, perhaps, still exist who believe that it is of no importance to explore the unknown polar regions. This, of course, shows ignorance. . . . The history of the human race is a continual struggle from darkness toward light. . . . Man wants to know, and when he ceases to do so, he is no longer man.[71]

Notes

Introduction: The Attraction of the Poles

1. Sarah Moss, *The Frozen Ship: The Histories and Tales of Polar Exploration*. New York: BlueBridge, 2006, pp. ix–x.
2. Quoted in Francis Leopold M'Clintock, *The Voyage of the Fox*. Philadelphia: J.T. Lloyd, 1860, p. 119.
3. David Mountfield, *A History of Polar Exploration*. New York: Dial, 1976, p. 11.
4. Clive Holland, ed., *Farthest North: Endurance and Adventure in the Quest for the North Pole*. New York: Carroll and Graf, 1999, pp. 1–2.

Chapter One: The Earliest Arctic Voyagers

5. Moss, *The Frozen Ship*, p. 1.
6. Pliny the Elder, *Natural History*, in *Pliny the Elder: Natural History: A Selection*, trans. John H. Healy. New York: Penguin, 1991, p. 34.
7. Anthony Brandt, ed., *The North Pole: A Narrative History*. Washington, DC: National Geographic, 2005, p. 3.
8. L.P. Kirwan, *A History of Polar Exploration*. New York: Norton, 1960, pp. 4–5.
9. Denis O'Donoghue, trans., *Voyage of St. Brendan the Navigator*, Lampeter, UK: University of Wales, Lampeter. www.lamp.ac.uk/celtic/elibrary/translations/nsb.htm.

10. O'Donoghue, *Voyage of St. Brendan the Navigator*.
11. Moss, *The Frozen Ship*, pp. 3–4.
12. Quoted in Farley Mowat, *The Polar Passion: The Quest for the North Pole*. Boston: Little, Brown, 1989, pp. 21–22.
13. Ohthere, "The Voyage of Ohthere, from King Alfred's *Orosius*," commentary by Amanda Graham, Yukon College. http://ycdl4.yukoncollege.yk.ca/~agraham//nost202/ottar.htm.

Chapter Two: Quests for the Northern Passages

14. Kirwan, *A History of Polar Exploration*, p. 11.
15. Moss, *The Frozen Ship*, p. 5.
16. Quoted in Mountfield, *A History of Polar Exploration*, p. 28.
17. Mountfield, *A History of Polar Exploration*, p. 32.
18. Clements R. Markham, *A Life of John Davis*. New York: Dodd, Mead, 1889, p. 71.
19. Mountfield, *A History of Polar Exploration*, p. 38.
20. Ralph K. Andrist, *Heroes of Polar Exploration*. New York: American Heritage, 1962, p. 45.
21. Quoted in Holland, *Farthest North*, pp. 27–28.
22. Pierre Berton, *Arctic Grail: The Quest for the Northwest Passage and the North*

Pole, 1818–1909. New York: Lyons, 2000, pp. 20–21.

Chapter Three: Search for the Southern Continent

23. Kirwin, *A History of Polar Exploration*, pp. 11–12.
24. Anthony Brandt, ed., *The South Pole: A Historical Reader*. Washington, DC: National Geographic, 2004, p. xi.
25. Quoted in Walker Chapman, ed., *Antarctic Conquest: The Great Explorers in Their Own Words*. New York: Bobbs-Merrill, 1965, p. 6.
26. Quoted in Kirwin, *A History of Polar Exploration*, pp. 42–43.
27. Quoted in Brandt, *The South Pole*, p. 8.
28. Quoted in Chapman, *Antarctic Conquest*, p. 23.
29. Brandt, *The South Pole*, pp. 11–12.
30. Quoted in Brandt, *The South Pole*, p. 22.
31. Quoted in Michael H. Rosove, ed., *Let Heroes Speak: Antarctic Explorers, 1772–1922*. Annapolis: Naval Institute Press, 2000, p. 5.
32. Quoted in Chapman, *Antarctic Conquest*, p. 42.
33. Quoted in Chapman, *Antarctic Conquest*, pp. 43–44.
34. Quoted in Chapman, *Antarctic Conquest*, p. 48.
35. Quoted in Kirwin, *A History of Polar Exploration*, p. 115.

Chapter Four: The Contest for the North Pole

36. Moss, *The Frozen Ship*, p. 19.
37. Brandt, *The North Pole*, p. 369.
38. Brandt, *The North Pole*, p. 371.
39. Quoted in Holland, *Farthest North*, p. 201.
40. Brandt, *The North Pole*, p. 390.
41. Quoted in Fergus Fleming, *Ninety Degrees North: The Quest for the North Pole*. New York: Grove, 2001, p. 308.
42. Quoted in Berton, *Arctic Grail*, p. 581.
43. Quoted in Brandt, *The North Pole*, p. 402.
44. Quoted in Holland, *Farthest North*, p. 206.
45. Fleming, *Ninety Degrees North*, pp. 365–66.
46. Quoted in Fleming, *Ninety Degrees North*, p. 387.
47. Holland, *Farthest North*, p. 219.

Chapter Five: Antarctica in the Heroic Age

48. John Maxtone-Graham, *Safe Return Doubtful: The Heroic Age of Polar Exploration*. New York: Scribners, 2000, p. 10.
49. Quoted in Rosove, *Let Heroes Speak*, p. 115.
50. Quoted in Rosove, *Let Heroes Speak*, p. 84.
51. Maxtone-Graham, *Safe Return Doubtful*, p. 193.
52. Quoted in Rosove, *Let Heroes Speak*, p. 83.
53. Rosove, *Let Heroes Speak*, p. 153.
54. Quoted in Rosove, *Let Heroes Speak*, p. 154.
55. Quoted in Diana Preston, *A First Rate Tragedy: Robert Falcon Scott and the Race to the South Pole*. Boston; Houghton Mifflin, 2001, p. 127.
56. Quoted in Chapman, *Antarctic Conquest*, p. 240.
57. Roald Amundsen, *The South Pole: An Account of the Norwegian Antarctic Expedition in the* Fram, *1910–1912*, Part II. New York: Cooper Square, 2001, p. 121.

58. Quoted in Preston, *A First Rate Tragedy*, p. 184.
59. Quoted in Preston, *A First Rate Tragedy*, p. 202.
60. Quoted in Preston, *A First Rate Tragedy*, p. 204.
61. Quoted in Preston, *A First Rate Tragedy*, p. 213.
62. Susan Solomon, *The Coldest March: Scott's Final Antarctic Expedition*. New Haven: Yale University Press, 2001, pp. 293–94, 297.
63. Quoted in Rosove, *Let Heroes Speak*, p. 197.

Chapter Six: The Age of Mechanized Exploration
64. Holland, *Farthest North*, p. 223.

65. Quoted in Holland, *Farthest North*, pp. 143–44.
66. C.V. Glimes, *Polar Aviation*. Milwaukee: E.M. Hale, 1967, p. viii.
67. Quoted in Glimes, *Polar Aviation*, p. 43.
68. Quoted in Glimes, *Polar Aviation*, p. 105.
69. Quoted in Chapman, *Antarctic Conquest*, pp. 299–300.
70. Quoted in Rosove, *Let Heroes Speak*, p. 242.

Epilogue: To Conquer the Unknown: Modern Polar Research
71. Quoted in Glimes, *Polar Aviation*, p. 1.

For More Information

Author's Note: Hundreds of readable books about polar explorers and their expeditions, some by the explorers themselves, have appeared in the last century or so. Of the more than fifty used in writing this volume, those cited below represent a sampling of some of the more comprehensive or useful ones.

Books

Roald Amundsen, *The South Pole: An Account of the Norwegian Antarctic Expedition in the* Fram, *1910–1912*. New York: Cooper Square, 2001. Amundsen, one of the greatest polar explorers, tells his own gripping story.

Pierre Berton, *Arctic Grail: The Quest for the Northwest Passage and the North Pole, 1818–1909*. New York: Lyons, 2000. A huge, well-written volume that covers all the major explorers and expeditions of the era mentioned in the title.

Anthony Brandt, ed., *The North Pole: A Narrative History*. Washington, DC: National Geographic, 2005. This excellent resource combines eye-witness accounts by polar explorers with Brandt's expert background information and commentary.

Anthony Brandt, ed., *The South Pole: A Historical Reader*. Washington, DC: National Geographic, 2004. Similar to Brandt's *North Pole* (see above) but concentrates on Antarctic explorers.

Walker Chapman, ed., *Antarctic Conquest: The Great Explorers in Their Own Words*. New York: Bobbs-Merrill, 1965. A collection of dozens of primary source documents by and about the great explorers who searched for the legendary southern continent.

James P. Delgado, *Across the Top of the World: The Quest for the Northwest Passage*. New York: Checkmark, 1999. A thorough discussion of the subject, accompanied by many photos, maps, and diagrams.

Fergus Fleming, *Ninety Degrees North: The Quest for the North Pole*. New York: Grove, 2001. Fleming delivers a fascinating study of the many expeditions to the North Pole during the 1800s and 1900s.

Clive Holland, ed., *Farthest North: Endurance and Adventure in the Quest for the North Pole*. New York: Carroll and Graf, 1999. A fact-filled synopsis of the major Arctic polar expeditions.

John Maxtone-Graham, *Safe Return Doubtful: The Heroic Age of Polar Exploration*. New York: Scribners, 2000. One of the better books about the heroic age, in which numerous polar explorers risked their lives, and some lost them.

Sarah Moss, *The Frozen Ship: The Histories and Tales of Polar Exploration*. New York: BlueBridge, 2006. A brief but useful overview of the major Arctic and Antarctic expeditions.

David Mountfield, *A History of Polar Exploration*. New York: Dial, 1976. Though now somewhat dated, Mountfield's overview of the subject remains a comprehensive and useful reference work.

Diana Preston, *A First Rate Tragedy: Robert Falcon Scott and the Race to the South Pole*. Boston: Houghton Mifflin, 2001. Preston, a historian, presents a well-written account of the famous contest for the South Pole and Robert Scott's sad fate.

Michael H. Rosove, ed., *Let Heroes Speak: Antarctic Explorers, 1772–1922*. Annapolis: Naval Institute Press, 2000. One of the better compilations of eyewitness accounts of polar exploration.

Ernest Shackleton, *South: The Last Antarctic Expedition of Shackleton and the Endurance*. New York: Lyons, 1998. Shackleton's own recollections of perhaps his most famous expedition.

Susan Solomon, *The Coldest March: Scott's Final Antarctic Expedition*. New Haven, CT: Yale University Press, 2001. A detailed, engrossing study of Scott's ill-fated polar trek and untimely death, including modern evidence that his death was caused by abnormally freezing temperatures.

Clint Willis, ed., *Ice: Stories of Survival from Polar Explorations*. New York: Thunder's Mouth, 1999. Several of the greatest polar explorers tell about their experiences.

Websites

Antarctica, the Continent of Wonder (http://library.thinkquest.org/28779). This excellent site maintained by ThinkQuest contains numerous links to all sorts of information about the ice-covered southernmost continent.

Arctic Passage (www.pbs.org/wgbh/nova/arctic). This PBS *Nova* site contains much useful information about two important polar explorers—Roald Amundsen and John Franklin.

Beaufort Gyre Exploration Project (www.whoi.edu/beaufortgyre/history.html). A comprehensive site maintained by Woods Hole Oceanographic Institution that contains numerous links to concise articles about polar exploration.

North Pole Environmental Observatory (http://psc.apl.washington.edu/northpole). A link provided by the National Science Foundation that takes the reader directly to the observatory, where he or she can check out the weather there, watch webcams, or link up with various scientific organizations. Highly recommended.

Quest for the Northwest Passage, 19th Century (www.whoi.edu/beaufort gyre/history/history_nwpassage .html). A link from the Beaufort Gyre Exploration Project (see above) that tells about some of the explorers who searched for the Northwest Passage in the early-to-mid-1800s.

South Pole.com (www.south-pole .com/homepage.html). A useful site dedicated to the many explorers who launched expeditions to Antarctica over the years.

St. Brendan, Sailor, Explorer, and Discoverer (www.whatdoyaknow.com/ Age%20of%20Discovery/St_Brendan/ Brendan-home.htm). Whatdoyaknow .com provides this concise, easy-to-read overview of the Atlantic voyages of St. Brendan and his Irish monks.

Index

Muscovy Company, 36

N
Nansen, Fridtjof, 91
Nobile, Umberto, 82
    route of, *53*
Nordenskiold, Otto, 65
    route of, *53*
Norge (airship), *82*
North Pole
    early attempts to reach, 52, 54
    environment of, 11–12
    first expedition to reach, 63
    first flight to, 83
    Peary claims to have reached,
      60
    territorial claims on, 88
Northwest Passage, *29*, 29–30,
    31

O
Oates, Lawrence, 73, 74
On the Ocean (Pytheas), 19
Operation Highjump (1946),
    85, 89
Ottar (Ohthere, Viking trader),
    25

P
Palmer, Nathaniel, 51
Parker, Herschel, 57
Parry, William E., 40
Peary, Robert E., *58*, 58–60, *61*
    claim of reaching North Pole,
      61, 63
    navigational errors of, 62
    notes of, *62*
    rivalry between Cook and, 54
    route of, *53*

Peter the Great (czar of Russia), 36
Le Petit Journal (magazine), *56*
Plaisted, Ralph, *86*, 86–87
Pliny the Elder, 19
Polar regions
    unique features of, 11–12
    See also North Pole; South
      Pole
Princess Charlotte (ship), 12–13
Ptolemy, 41
Pytheas, 17, 19–20

R
Resolution (Cook's ship), *48*
Roche, Anthony de la, 46
Roosevelt, Franklin D., 85
Ross, James Clark, 40
Ross, John, 40
Royal Society (U.K.), 45–46

S
Scott, Robert Falcon, 65, 67–68,
    73–74, 77
Shackleton, Ernest, 69–71, *70*,
    70, 76
Siculus, Diodorus, 20
Solomon, Susan, 75
South Pole
    environment of, 11–12
    first expedition to reach, 73
    first permanent base at, 89
Spitzbergen Islands, 36, 38

T
Temperatures, at North *vs.*
    South Pole, 12
Terra Nova expedition, 73
Thorgisl (Viking), 23–25, 26
Tierra del Fuego, 44

Picture Credits

Cover: © Stapleton Collection/Corbis

Thomas J. Abercrombie/National Geographic/Getty Images, 13

AP Images, 55

Joseph H. Bailey/National Geographic/Getty Images, 61, 62

© Bettmann/Corbis, 58 (both), 86

David Boyer/National Geographic/Getty Images (top), 9

© DeA Picture Library/Art Resource, NY, 33

The Discovery of Greenland, from *Harper's Weekly*, Vol. 19, p.780-81, 1875 (engraving) (b&w photo), American School, (19th century)/Private Collection/The Bridgeman Art Library, 26

Erik the Red (950-1003/04) sets sail for Greenland, illustration from *The Book of Discovery* by T.C. Bridges, published 1931 (colour litho), Reid, Stephen Reid (1873-1948)/Private Collection/The Bridgeman Art Library, 24

© Werner Forman/Art Resource, NY, 8 (bottom left)

Gale/Cengage Learning, 31, 42, 53, 67

© HIP/Art Resource, 21, 56

Hulton Archive/Getty Images, 8 (bottom right), 9 (bottom), 68, 70, 75

© Hulton-Deutsch Collection/Corbis, 84

The last voyage of Henry Hudson, illustration from *Hutchinson's Story of the British Nation*, c.1923 (litho), Collier, John (1850-1934) (after)/Private Collection/The Stapleton Collection/The Bridgeman Art Library, 37

Mansell/Time & Life Pictures/Getty Images, 71, 76, 81

© Maps.com/Corbis, 18

© Momatiuk-Eastcott/Corbis, 50

© NASA/Corbis, 29

© North Wind Picture Archives, 35

Peary's expedition to the North Pole, English School, (20th century)/Private Collection/© Look and Learn/The Bridgeman Art Library, 65

Pictorial Parade/Getty Images, 82

Popperfoto/Getty Images, 79

Portrait of Captain Cook, c.1800 (copy of portrait in the National Maritime Museum, Greenwich, England), Dance Holland, Nathaniel (1735-1811) (after)/© National Library of Australia, Canberra, Australia/The Bridgeman Art Library, 47

The *Resolution* Beating Through the Ice with the *Discovery* in the most Imminent Danger in the Distance, from 'Views in the South Seas', pub. 1792 (etching), Webber, John (1750-93)/Private Collection/The Bridgeman Art Library, 48

Sir Francis Drake, Lane, Samuel (1780-1859)/The Crown Estate/The Bridgeman Art Library, 45

© The Stapleton Collection/Art Resource, NY, 32

Stock Montage/Getty Images (top), 8

© Topham/The Image Works, 66

The Whaling Fleet of Sir Samuel Standidge, Hull School of Painting, 1769 (oil on canvas), English School, (18th century)/Ferens Art Gallery, Hull Museums, UK/The Bridgeman Art Library, 38

Gordon Wiltsie/National Geographic/Getty Images, 14

About the Author

In addition to his numerous acclaimed volumes on ancient civilizations, historian Don Nardo has written and edited several studies of scientific discoveries and phenomena (including *The Extinction of the Dinosaurs, Cloning, Black Holes, Extraterrestrial Life, Comets and Asteroids, Volcanoes,* and *Climate Change*) and biographies of noted scientists (including Galileo, Tycho Brahe, and Charles Darwin). Nardo also composes and arranges orchestral music. He lives with his wife Christine in Massachusetts.